Touched by an E-mail

D0404358

Touched by an E-mail

Bridge-Logos *Publishers*

North Brunswick, New Jersey 08902 USA

Bridge-Logos, 1999, All Rights Reserved; Bridge-Logos disclaims any and all rights to passages in this publication obtained from e-mail transmissions that were forwarded to it and did not identify the author. Bridge-Logos considers such materials as being in the public domain.

TOUCHED BY AN E-MAIL
by Denny Mog
Copyright © 1999 by Bridge-Logos Publishers
Library of Congress Catalog Card Number: 99-64059
International Standard Book Number: 0-88270-773-6

Published by:

Bridge-Logos *Publishers*
1300 Airport Road, Suite E
North Brunswick, NJ 08902
http://www.bridgelogos.com

Printed in the United States of America. All rights reserved.
Under International Copyright Law, no part of this publication may be reproduced, stored or transmitted by any means—electronic, mechanical, photographic (photocopy), recording, or otherwise—without written permission from the Publisher.

Touched by an E-mail

"The heavens declare the glory
of God; and the skies proclaim
the work of His hands. Day
after day they pour forth speech;
night after night they display
their knowledge. There is no
speech or language where their
voice is not heard. Their voice
goes out into all the earth,
their words to the ends of the world."

Psalm 19:1-4

Contents

I Tears and Laughter with Children

II Tears and Laughter in Church

III Tears and Laughter When God Speaks

IV Tears and Laughter at Home

V Tears and Laughter When Praying

VI Tears and Laughter in School

VII Tears and Laughter When Working

VIII Tears and Laughter at the Pearly Gates

There's a story in this book about a mother who is attempting to teach her young daughter The Lord's Prayer. On her first solo attempt to recite the prayer, the girl almost had it right, except for one phrase — "...and deliver us some e-mail."

For many of us, the little girl's mistake is easily understood, for our children today are experiencing — as are we —the expectations that accompany life in the Information Age. We have routinely come to accept and expect almost instantaneous world-wide communication. Electronic mail – e-mail – is a rapidly spreading phenomenon, and the term "dot com" trips lightly from our tongue. Children and adults now scurry to their computers to look for their latest e-mail, just as we used to run to the mail box at the front of our homes to check for the Sears "Wish Book" or the latest letter from Aunt Sage. Now, the book, as well as the letter, can pop up in our electronic mailboxes, and it's all courtesy of the World Wide Web and the Internet of which it is a part.

Estimates vary but most experts say that from 50 to 70 million people will be connected to the Internet by the year 2000. Those folks will be surfing through some 300 million pages of information maintained on more than four million Web sites. Even now, more than one million pages of Web-based information are born daily and Internet traffic—people like you and me sending and receiving information—is said to be doubling in volume every 100 days.

Is it any wonder then that the people of God would latch on to the Internet and begin to use it almost miraculously to reach into the homes and businesses of untold millions around the world? The electronic or "virtual" missionaries of the World Wide Web are disseminating the Lord's good news today in a way that simply dwarfs the efforts of the evangelicals who preceded them. We now have immediate access to Bibles and Bible commentaries of every fashion. We can plug into religious newspapers and magazines, read electronic religious texts and delve into informational sites maintained by almost every organized religion or religious group that exists. Folks who want to read about God, learn about God or even argue about God have had laid before them on the Internet a spiritual smorgasbord of thousands upon thousands of pages of information from which to choose.

Millions of God's people now sit before computers and form a virtual neighborhood—an electronic Saturday night social—where they share funny stories or inspirational vignettes with their friends and sometimes with people they don't even know. Sharing seems to be basic to the nature of this electronic medium. There's not a day goes by that I don't receive from someone a joke, a poem, a devotional or an inspirational story, most of which are culled from religious Web sites. The messages are almost always uplifting and more often than not I forward them through my e-mail to other friends and associates. The messages bounce around the country like inspirational chain letters that carry only the promise of a laugh, a moment of peace or reflection, or a gentle reminder of the sovereignty of our God.

While the context is not the same and I wouldn't begin to equate the Internet with heaven, the opening verses in Psalm 19 describe for me a heavenly outreach that is the Christian World Wide Web. David says in Verses 1-4: "The heavens declare the glory of God; and the skies proclaim the work of His hands. Day after day they pour forth speech; night after night they display their knowledge. There is no speech or language where their voice is not heard. Their voice goes out into all the earth, their words to the ends of the world."

This book is a collection of e-mail messages I've received from web-users and various corners of the Internet. From whom such delightful items originate is difficult to tell. All that appear in this book have been anonymously cast upon the Web by people who must simply receive their joy by thinking and writing about God. The items are at times laughingly clever. At other times, they are pensive, sad, and they often convey a simple truthfulness that we might have overlooked. But always, they reveal a vivid understanding of what our lives and our relationships with God were designed to be. That's why I think God might like this book. God always loves us, but He probably loves us best when we are thinking about Him.

The book is subtitled "Tears and Laughter from the Web" and I've categorized the many "tears and laughter" entries in specific subject areas like church, children, praying and so on. It's a book you can pick up and put down and then pick up later. Or it's a book you can read straight through from beginning to end.

But most of all, it's a book that probably won't stop with you. I can almost promise that you will find yourselves passing on its stories to your friends and family members. I hope so.

Dennis D. Mog
June 1999

Section I

Touched
by an
E-mail

Tears & Laughter with Children

I Want to be Six Again

I want to go to school and have snack time, recess, gym, and field trips.

I want to sail sticks across a fresh mud puddle and make waves with rocks.

I want to be happy because I don't know what makes me sad.

I want to believe that everything is possible.

I want television to be something I watch for fun, not something I use to escape from the things I should be doing.

I want to think M&Ms are better than money because you can eat them.

I want to think the world is fair and everyone in it is honest and good.

I want to wonder what I'll do when I grow up.

I want to think that everyone, including myself, will live forever.

I want to be oblivious to the complexity of life.

I want to be naïve enough to think that if I'm happy, so is everyone else.

I want to worry about things like what can I possibly use for the snowman's mouth.

I want to be six again.

Kids Ask God

Why isn't Mrs. God's name in the Bible? Weren't you married to her when you wrote it?

How come you only have 10 rules and our school has millions?

Where does yesterday go? Do you have it?

When you made the first man did he work as good as we do now?

5

It's Not Empty

Some time ago, a father punished his young daughter for wasting a roll of gold wrapping paper. Money was tight, and dad became angry when the child tried to decorate a box to put under the Christmas tree.

Nevertheless, the little girl brought the gift to the father the next morning and said, "This is for you, daddy." He was embarrassed by his earlier overreaction, but his anger flared again when he found the box was empty. He yelled at her, "Don't you know that when you give someone a present, there's supposed to be something inside of it?"

The little looked up at him with tears in her eyes and said, "Oh, daddy, it's not empty. I blew kisses into the box...all for you, daddy."

The father was crushed. He put his arms around his little girl, and he begged her forgiveness. He kept that gold box by his bed for years. Whenever he was discouraged, he would take out an imaginary kiss and remember the love of the child who put it there.

"Yes dear, every word"

A dad had a habit of always complaining about the food his wife placed before him at family meals. After grumbling, he would ask the blessing.

One day after his usual combination complaint-prayer, his little daughter asked, "Daddy, does God hear us when we pray?"

"Why, of course," he replied. "He hears us every time we pray."

She thought about his answer a moment, then asked, "Does he hear everything we say the rest of the time, too?"

"Yes, dear, every word," the dad said, encouraged that he had inspired his daughter to be curious about spiritual matters. But then his pride turned to humility when his daughter then asked:

"Then which does God believe?"

When You Were Born

When you were born, you cried
and the world rejoiced.
Live your life in such a way that
when you die,
The world cries and you rejoice.

My Dear Child

I can teach you things, but I cannot make you learn.

I can give you directions, but I cannot be there to lead you.

I can allow you freedom, but I cannot account for it.

I can take you to church, but I cannot make you believe.

I can teach you right from wrong, but I cannot always decide for you.

I can buy you beautiful clothes, but I cannot make you beautiful inside.

I can offer you advice, but I cannot accept it for you.

I can give you love, but I cannot force it upon you.

I can teach you to respect, but I cannot force you to show honor.

I can advise you about friends, but cannot choose them for you.

I can advise you about sex, but I cannot keep you pure.

I can tell you about the facts of life, but I cannot build your reputation.

I can tell you about drink, but I can't say "no" for you.

I can warn you about drugs, but I can't prevent you from using them.

I can tell you about lofty goals, but I can't achieve them for you.

I can teach you about kindness, but I can't force you to be gracious.

I can warn you about sins, but I cannot make you moral.

I can love you as a child, but I cannot place you in God's family.

I can pray for you, but I cannot make you walk with God.

I can teach you about Jesus, but I cannot make Jesus your Lord.

I can tell you how to live, but I cannot give you eternal life.

I can love you unconditionally all my life, and I will.

Always, Mom

Plain Vanilla

Many years ago when an ice cream sundae cost much less than today, little Jamie entered a coffee shop and sat at a table. As a waitress put a glass of water in front of him, the little boy asked,

"How much is an ice cream sundae?"

"Fifty cents," replied the waitress.

The little boy pulled his hand out of his pocket and studied a number of coins in it. "How much is a dish of plain vanilla?" he asked.

Some other people were now waiting for a table, and the waitress was impatient. "Thirty-five cents," she said angrily.

Jamie counted his coins again. "Ok," he said, "I'll have the plain ice cream."

The waitress brought the ice cream and walked away. The boy finished, paid the cashier, and departed. When the waitress came back, she swallowed hard at what she saw. There, placed neatly beside the empty dish, were two nickels and five pennies—her tip.

The Most Beautiful Flower

The park bench was deserted as I sat down to read beneath the long, straggly branches of an old willow tree. Disillusioned by life with good reason to frown, I felt like the world was intent on dragging me down.

And if that weren't enough to ruin my day, a young boy out of breath approached me, all tired from play. He stood right before me with his head tilted down and said with great excitement, "Look what I found."

In his hand was a flower and what a pitiful sight, with its pedals all worn—not enough rain, or too little light. Wanting him to take his dead flower and go off to play, I faked a small smile and then drifted away.

But instead of retreating he sat next to my side
and placed the flower to his nose and declared with
surprise, "It sure smells pretty and it's beautiful, too.
That's why I picked it. Here, it's for you."

The weed before me was dying or dead. Not
vibrant of colors, orange, yellow or red. But I knew I
must take it, or he might never leave. So I reached
for the flower, and replied, "Just what I need."

But instead of him placing the flower in my
hand, he held it in mid-air without reason or plan. It
was then that I noticed for the very first time that
weed-toting boy could not see. He was blind.

I heard my voice quiver, tears shone like the sun
as I thanked him for picking the very best one.
"You're welcome," he smiled, and then ran off to play,
unaware of the impact he'd had on my day.

I sat there and wondered how he managed to
see a self-pitying woman beneath an old tree.
How did he know of my self-indulged plight?

Perhaps from his heart, he'd been blessed with true sight.

Through the eyes of a blind child at last I could see the problem was not with the world; the problem was me. And for all those times I myself had been blind, I vowed to see beauty, and appreciate every second that's mine.

And then I held that wilted flower up to my nose and breathed in the fragrance of a beautiful rose and smiled as that young boy, another weed in his hand, was about to change the life of an unsuspecting old man.

The Starfish

A vacationing businessman was walking along a beach when he saw a young boy. Along the shore were many starfish that had been washed up by the tide and were sure to die before the tide returned.

The boy was walking slowly along the shore and occasionally reached down and tossed the beached starfish back into the ocean. The businessman, hoping to teach the boy a little lesson in common sense, walked up to the boy and said, "I have been watching what you are doing, son. You have a good heart, and I know you mean well, but do you realize how many beaches there are around here and how many starfish are dying on every beach every day? Surely such an industrious and kind-hearted boy as yourself could find something better to do with your time. Do you really think that what you are doing is going to make a difference?"

The boy looked up at the man, and then looked down at a starfish by his feet. He picked up the starfish, and as he gently tossed it back into the ocean, he said, "It makes a difference to that one."

You Are Setting an Example

There are little eyes upon you,
  And they're watching night and day.
There are little ears that quickly
  Take in everything you say.
There are little hands all eager
  To do anything you do;
And a little boy who's dreaming
  Of the day he'll be like you.
You're the fellow's idol;
  You're the wisest of the wise.
In his mind about you
  No suspicions ever rise.
He believes in you devoutly
  Hold all you say and do.
He will say and do in your way

When he's grown up just like you.
There's a wide-eyed little fellow
    Who believes you're always right.
And his eyes are always opened,
    And he watches day and night.
You are setting an example
    Everyday in all you do
For the little boy who's waiting
    To grow up to be like you.

Where God Ain't

He was just a little lad,
and on the week's first day,
He was wandering home from Sunday School,
and dawdling on the way.

He scuffed his shoes into the grass;
he found a caterpillar;
He found a fluffy milkweed pod,
and blew out all the filler.

A bird's nest in a tree o'er head
so wisely placed on high,
Was just another wonder
that caught his eagle eye.
A neighbor watched his zigzag course

and hailed him from the lawn;
Asked him where he'd been that day,
and what was going on.

"I've been to Bible school," he said
and turned a piece of sod.
He picked up a wiggly worm and said,
"I've learned a lot from God."

"M'm a very fine way," the neighbor said,
"for a boy to spend his time.
If you tell me where God is,
I'll give you a brand new dime."

Quick as a flash his answer came.
Nor were his accents faint.
"I'll give you a dollar, mister,
if you tell me where God ain't!"

Contaminated Water

A young mother decided it was time that her three sons be baptized. So after weeks of appropriate instructions, the three boys were on their way to church for the ceremony where they would have their sins washed away.

The youngest son was particularly apprehensive and when his mother asked him what he was thinking about, his reply was a question.

"Mom," he said, "I want to go first."

"Why," she asked.

"Because I don't want to be baptized in water that has all my brothers' sins floating around in it."

And Fly More Kites

If I had my child to rear over again, I'd finger paint more and point the finger less.

I would do less correcting and more connecting.

I'd take my eyes off my watch, and watch with
my eyes.

I would care to know less and know to care
more.

I'd take more hikes and fly more kites.

I'd stop playing serious and seriously play.

I would run through more fields and gaze more
at stars.

I'd do more hugging and less tugging.

I'd build self-esteem first, and the house later.

I would be firm less often, and affirm much
  more.
I'd teach less about the love of power, and more
  about the power of love.

A Small Child's Advice to Her Parents

My hands are small. Please don't expect perfection whenever I make a bed, draw a picture or throw a ball.

My eyes have not seen the world as yours have. Please let me explore it at my own level without unnecessary restrictions.

Housework will always be there, but I will be little only for a short time. Please take time to explain about this wonderful world.

My feelings are tender. Please be sensitive to my needs. Treat me as you would like to be treated.

I am a special gift from God. Treasure me as God intended, holding me accountable for my actions, giving me guidelines to live by, and disciplining me in a loving manner.

I need your encouragement to grow, so go easy on the criticism.

Try to correct my behavior without criticizing me as a person.

Give me the freedom to make decisions. Permit me to fail, so I can learn from my mistakes. I want to be prepared to make the kind of decisions life will require of me as an adult.

Don't do jobs over that I have done. This makes me feel that my efforts don't quite measure up to your expectations. I know it's difficult, but please don't compare me with my brother or sister.

Please don't be afraid to leave for a weekend together. Kids need vacations from parents, just as parents need to get away occasionally.

This is also a great way to show us kids that your marriage is very special.

Please set a good example by taking me to church and Sunday School regularly. I enjoy learning about God.

Nail Holes in the Fence

There was a little boy with a bad temper. His father gave him a bag of nails and told him that every time he lost his temper he was to hammer a nail in the backyard fence.

The first day the boy had driven 37 nails into the fence. But each day the number of nails became fewer and fewer. He discovered it was easier to hold his temper than to drive those nails in the fence.

Finally the day came when the boy didn't lose his temper once. He told his father about it, and the father suggested that the boy now pull out one nail for each day that he was able to hold his temper. The days passed and the boy was finally able to tell his father that all the nails were gone. The father took his son by the hand and led him to the fence.

He said, "You have done well, my son, but look at the holes in the fence. The fence will never be the same. When you say things in anger, they leave a scar just like these holes. You can put a knife in a man and draw it out. But it won't make any difference how many times you say I'm sorry. The wound is still there. And a verbal wound can be just as bad as a physical one.

Love Leaves the Dust

If I live in a house of spotless beauty with everything in its place, but have not love, I am a housekeeper, not a homemaker.

If I have time for waxing, polishing, and decorative achievements, but have not love, my children learn cleanliness, not Godliness.

Love leaves the dust in search of a child's laugh.

Love smiles at the tiny fingerprints on a newly cleaned window.

Love wipes away the tears before it wipes up spilled milk.

Love picks up the child before it picks up the toys.

Love is present through the trials.

Love reprimands, reproves, and is responsive. Love crawls with the baby, walks with the toddler, runs with the child, then stands aside to let the youth walk into adulthood.

Love is the key that opens salvation's message to a child's heart.

Before I became a mother I took glory in my house of perfection.

Now I glory in God's perfection of my child.

As a mother, there is much I must teach my child, but the greatest of all is love

But He Can't Run and Play

An eight-year-old boy went to a pet store with his dad to buy a puppy.

The store manager showed them to a pen where five little puppies were huddled together. After a while, the boy noticed one of the litter all by itself in an adjacent pen.

The boy asked, "Why is that puppy all alone?"

The manager explained, "That puppy was born with a bad leg and would be crippled for life, so we're going to have to put him to sleep."

"You're going to kill this little puppy?" the boy said sadly.

"You have to realize that this puppy would never be able to run and play with a boy like you," the manager said.

After a short conversation with his boy, the dad told the manager that they wanted to buy the puppy with the bad leg,

"For the same amount of money, you could have one of the healthy ones," the manager said. "Why do you want this one?"

To answer the manager's question, the boy bent over and pulled up the pants on his right leg and exposed a brace underneath. He said, "Mister, I want this one because I know what he's going through."

Why I Believe In God

Some third-graders were asked to explain God.

One of God's main jobs is making people. He makes these to put in place of the ones that die so that there will be enough people to take care of things here on earth. He doesn't make grownups, just babies. I think that's because they are smaller and easier to make. That way He doesn't have to take up His valuable time teaching them to talk and walk. He can just leave that up to the mothers and fathers. I think it works out pretty good.

God's second most important job is listening to prayers. An awful lot of this goes on as some people, like preachers, pray other times besides bedtime. God doesn't have time to listen to the radio or TV on account of this. As He hears everything, not only prayers, there must be a terrible lot of noise in His ears, unless He has thought of a way to turn it off.

God sees everything and hears everything and is everywhere. This keeps Him pretty busy. So you shouldn't go wasting His time by going over your parents' head to ask Him for something they said you shouldn't have.

Atheists are people who don't believe in God. I don't think there are any around here. At least there aren't any who come to our church.

Jesus is God's son. He used to do all the hard work, like walking on water and doing miracles and trying to teach people about God who didn't want to learn. They finally got tired of Him preaching to them and they crucified Him.

But He was good and kind like His father and He told His father that they didn't know what they were doing and to forgive them. And God said OK. His dad (God) appreciated everything He had done and all His hard work on earth. So God told Him he didn't have to go out on the road anymore. He could stay in heaven. So He did.

And now He helps His dad out by listening to prayers and seeing which things are important to God to take care of and which ones He can take care of Himself without having to bother God. He's like a secretary only more important, of course.

A Deal's A Deal

A young man had just received his driving permit. He asked his dad, a minister, if they could discuss the use of the family car. His father took him to his study and said to him, "I'll make a deal with you. You bring your grades up, study your Bible a little and get your hair cut and we'll talk about it."

About a month later, the young man came back and asked his dad if they could again discuss use of the car. The father said, "Son, I'm real proud of you. You have brought your grades up, you've studied the Bible diligently, but you didn't get your hair cut."

The young man waited a moment and replied,

"You know, Dad, I've been thinking about that. You know, Samson had long hair, Moses had long hair, Noah had long hair, and even Jesus had long hair."

To which his father replied, "Yes, and they walked every where they went."

Twinkies in the Park with God

There once was a little boy who wanted to meet with God. He knew it was a long trip to where God lived, so he packed his suitcase with Twinkies and a six-pack of root beer and he started his journey.

When he had gone about three blocks, he met an old woman. She was sitting in the park just staring at some pigeons. The boy sat down next to her and opened his suitcase. He was about to take a drink from his root beer when he noticed that the old lady looked hungry, so he offered her a Twinkie.

She gratefully accepted it and smiled at him. Her smile was so pretty that the boy wanted to see it again, so he offered her a root beer. Once again she smiled at him. The boy was delighted.

They sat there all afternoon eating and smiling, but they never said a word. As it grew dark, the boy realized how tired he was and got up to leave, but before he had gone more than a few steps, he turned around, ran back to the old woman and gave her a hug. He gave her the biggest smile ever.

When the boy opened the door to his own house a short time later, his mother was surprised by the look of joy on his face.

She asked him, "What did you do today that made you so happy?" "I had lunch with God," he replied. But before his mother could respond, he added, "You know what? She's got the most beautiful smile I've ever seen."

Meanwhile, the old woman, also radiant with joy, returned to her home.

Her son was stunned by the look of peace on her face and he asked,

"Mother, what did you do today that made you so happy?"

She replied, "I ate Twinkies in the park with God." But before her son responded, she added, "You know, he is much younger than I expected."

ABCs For Parents about their Kids

A — Always trust them to God.

B — Bring them to church.

C — Challenge them to high ideals.

D — Delight in their achievements.

E — Exalt the Lord in their presence.

F — Frown on evil.

G — Give them love.

H — Hear their problems.

I — Ignore not their childish fears.

J — Joyfully accept their apologies.

K — Keep their confidence.

L — Live a good example before them..

M — Make them your friends.

N — Never ignore their endless questions.

O — Open your home to their visits.

P — Pray for them by name.

Q — Quicken your interest in their spirituality.

R — Remember their needs.

S — Show them the way to salvation.

T — Teach them to work.

U — Understand they are still young.

V — Verify your statements.

W — Wean them from bad company.

X — Expect them to obey.

Y — Yearn for God's best for them.

Z — Zealously guide them in Biblical truth.

You Are My Sunshine

Like any good mother, when Karen found out that another baby was on the way, she did what she could do to help her three-year-old son, Michael, prepare for a new sister. They had found out that the baby was a girl, and day after day, night after night, Michael would put his head on Mommy's tummy and sing to his sister.

In time, the labor pains came. Soon it was every five minutes, then every one minute. But serious complications arose during delivery, and Karen found herself in hours of labor. Finally after a long struggle, Michael's little sister was born, but she was in serious condition.

The baby was placed in intensive care, but the pediatric specialist regretfully had to tell the parents,

"There is very little hope. Be prepared for the worst."

Michael kept begging his parents to let him see his sister. "I need to see her," he kept saying. After two weeks in intensive care, it appeared as if the end was near. But Michael kept begging to see his sister.

Kids were not allowed in intensive care, but Karen had made up her mind. If Michael didn't see his sister soon, he might never see her alive, She dressed Michael in an oversized gown and over the objections of a nurse, she brought him to his sister's bedside.

Michael gazed at the tiny infant and after a few moments, he began to sing. In the pure-hearted voice of a three-year old, Michael sang, "You are my sunshine, my only sunshine. You make me happy when skies are gray." Instantly, the baby girl seemed to respond. Her pulse rate began to calm and become steady.

"Keep on singing, Michael," encouraged Karen with tears in her eyes.

"You never know, dear, how much I love you, please don't take my sunshine away." As Michael sang to his sister, the baby's ragged, strained breathing became as smooth as a kitten's purr.

"Keep on singing, sweetheart," Karen said again. "The other night, dear, as I lay sleeping, I dreamed I held you in my arms." Michael's little sister began to relax. Healing rest seemed to sweep over her. "Keep on singing, Michael!"

Tears had now conquered the face of the bossy nurse. Karen was beside herself. Miraculously, Michael's baby sister went home the next day.

"Woman's Day" magazine called the event, "The Miracle of a Brother's Song." The hospital staff just called it a miracle. Karen called it a miracle of God.

Section II

Touched
by an
E-mail

Tears & Laughter in Church

A Living Bible

His name is Bill. He has wild hair, wears a tee shirt with holes in it, jeans and no shoes. This was literally his wardrobe for his entire four years of college. He is brilliant, kind of esoteric and very, very bright. He became a Christian while attending college.

Across the street from the campus is a well-dressed, very conservative church. They want to develop a ministry to the students, but are not sure how to go about it.

One Sunday, Bill decides to go to the church. He walks in with no shoes, jeans, tee shirt, and wild hair. The service has already started, so Bill starts down the aisle looking for a seat. The church is completely packed, and he can't find a seat. By now, people are really looking a bit uncomfortable, but no one says anything.

Bill gets closer and closer to the pulpit, and when he realizes there are no seats, he just squats down right on the carpet.

By now the people are really uptight, and the tension in the air is thick. About this time, the minister realizes that from the back of the church, a deacon is slowly making his way toward Bill. Now the deacon is in his eighties, has silver-gray hair, and a three-piece suit.

He's a godly man, very elegant, very dignified, very courtly. He walks with a cane and, as he starts walking toward the boy, everyone is saying to themselves that you can't blame him for what he's going to do.

How can you expect a man of his age and of his background to understand some college kid sitting on the floor. It takes a long time for the man to reach the boy. The church is utterly silent, except for the clicking of the man's cane. All eyes are focused on him.

The minister can't even begin preaching until the deacon does what he has to do. And now they see the elderly deacon drop his cane on the floor. With great difficulty he lowers himself and sits down next to Bill and worships with him so he won't be alone.

Everyone chokes up with emotion, When the minister regains control, he says, "What I'm about to preach, you will never remember. What you have just seen, you will never forget. Be careful how you live. You may be the only Bible some people will ever read."

The Children of Israel

Mrs. Jones, a Sunday School teacher, had just finished the day's lesson. It was now time for questions.

"Mrs. Jones," little Joey asked, "there's something I can't figure out."

"What's that, Joey?" she asked.

"Well, according to the Bible, the Children of Israel crossed the Red Sea, right?"

"Right."

"And the Children of Israel beat up the Philistines, right?"

"Yes, that's right," the teacher answered.

"And the Children of Israel built the temple, right?" And the Children of Israel fought the

Egyptians, and the Children of Israel fought the Romans, and the Children of Israel were always doing something important, right?"

"All that is right, too," Mrs. Jones agreed. "So what's your question?"

"What I want to know is this," said Joey. "What were all the grown-ups doing while all this was going on?"

The Fiery Sermon

A man tells this story about the time his pastor came to his home for a visit. The man was a church member, who had attended services regularly but suddenly stopped going. After some weeks went by, his pastor decided to visit him.

It was a chilly evening, and the pastor found the man at home sitting near a blazing fire. The man welcomed the pastor, guessing the reason for his visit, and invited him to sit in a big chair near the fireplace. The pastor made himself comfortable, but said nothing.

In silence he watched the play of the flames around the burning logs. After a few minutes, the pastor took the fire tongs, carefully picked up a brightly burning ember and placed it to one side of the hearth all alone. Still silent, he sat back in his chair.

The host watched in fascination. As the one lone ember's flame diminished, there was a brief glow and then its fire went out. Soon it was cold.

Not a word had been spoken since the initial greeting. Just before the pastor was about to leave, he picked up the cold, dead ember and placed it back in the middle of the fire. Immediately it began to glow once more with the light and the warmth of the burning coals around it.

As the pastor reached the door to leave, his host said, "Thank you so much for your visit and especially for the fiery sermon. I'll be back in church next Sunday."

The Forgotten Man

A pious man who had reached the age of 105 suddenly stopped going to church. Alarmed by the old man's absence after so many years of faithful attendance, the pastor went to visit him. He found him in excellent health, so the pastor asked, "How come after all these years we don't see you in services anymore?"

The old man looked around and lowered his voice. "I'll tell you, pastor," he whispered. "When I got to be 90 I expected God to take me any day.

But then I got to be 95, then 100, then 105. So I figured that God is very busy and must have forgotten about me...and I don't want to remind him."

Egg Money

A new minister had recently been married. Upon returning home from the honeymoon, the young wife turned to her husband with a box in her hand. She said to her husband, "Please promise dear that no matter what, you will never look in this box." It seemed like a strange request, but the minister agreed.

Twenty years went by and the seasoned minister was looking around in his closet. He came across the box which he had forgotten long ago.

He said to himself, "surely after all these years, it must be OK to peek inside." He opened the box and inside found $1200 and three eggs.

Just then his wife entered the room.

"I thought I asked you never to look inside?" she demands. Looking just a bit sheepish, the minister apologized to his wife, but then said that since he had peeked inside would she mind explaining the contents.

"Well," replied his wife, "If you must know, every time you preached a bad sermon, I put an egg in the box." The minister ponders this for a moment and rationalizes that he's been preaching for twenty years so three eggs was basically a very good record.

"That explains the eggs," he replied, "but what about the $1200?"

His wife explained, "Every time I got a dozen, I sold them."

Ten Dollars

Why is it that $10 looks so small at the grocery store, but so big at church?

A one-dollar bill and a one-hundred-dollar bill got folded together one day and began talking about their life experiences.

The one-hundred-dollar bill began to brag: "I've had a great life," he said. "I've been in all the big hotels. I've been in casinos and in the wallets of some of the most important executives. I've flown from one end of the country to the other."

In awe, the dollar bill responded humbly. "Gee, nothing like that has ever happened to me...but I have been to church a lot."

Ten Reasons Why I Never Wash

1. I was forced to wash as a child.

2. People who wash are hypocrites. They think they are cleaner than anyone else.

3. There are so many different kinds of soap. I can't decide which one is best.

4. I used to wash, but I got bored and stopped.

5. I wash only on special occasions, like Christmas and Easter.

6. None of my friends wash.

7. I'll start washing when I get older and dirtier.

8. I can't spare the time.

9.   The bathroom is never warm enough in winter or cool enough in summer.

10. People who make soap are only after your money.

He Had Their Attention

A young pastor tells this story.

We were traveling one summer in the mountains and my family and I always attend church on Sunday. One lazy Sunday we found our way to a little Methodist church. It was a very hot day and it seemed like the folks in the pews were nearly passed out. The preacher was going on and on until, all of a sudden, he said, "The best years of my life were spent in the arms of another man's wife."

The congregation let out a gasp, came to immediate attention, and the dozing deacon in the back row dropped his hymnbook. Then the preacher said, "It was my mother." The congregation tittered a little and managed to follow along as the sermon concluded. I filed this story away in my memory; a great way to regain the congregation's attention when it had been lost.

Sure enough, the next summer on a lazy Sunday, I was preaching and the members of the congregation seemed to be sinking lower and lower in their seats. Then I remembered my Methodist Church experience and I said in a booming voice, 'The best years of my life have been spent in the arms of another man's wife.'

Sure enough, I had their attention. One of the ushers in the back row sat up so fast he hit his head on the back of the pew in front of him. I had them. But you know something? I forgot what came next. All I could think to say was, 'And for the life of me, I can't remember her name.'

God's Light

One bright summer morning a little child stood in a great church. Sunlight streamed through the beautiful stained glass windows, And the figures in the windows of the servants of God were radiant with brilliant colors.

A little while later, the young girl was asked, "What is a saint?"

She replied, "A saint is a person who lets God's light shine through."

Return To Sender

A minister was opening his mail one morning. Drawing a single sheet of paper from an envelope, he found written on it only one word: "Fool."

The next Sunday, he announced during services, "I have known many people who have written letters and forgotten to sign their names. But this week I received a letter from someone who signed his name and had forgotten to write a letter."

There's One in Every Crowd

What do angels look like?
Like the little old lady who returned
   your wallet yesterday.
Like the taxi driver who told you that your eyes
   light up the world when you smile.
Like the small child who showed you
   the wonder in simple things.
Like the poor man who offered to
   share his lunch with you.
Like the rich man who showed you that it
   really is all possible if you only believe.
Like the stranger who just happened to come
   along when you had lost your way.
Like the friend who touched your heart
   when you didn't think you had one to touch.

Angels come in all sizes and shapes,
   all ages and skin types.
Some with freckles, some with dimples,
   some with wrinkles, some without.
They come disguised as friends, enemies,
   teachers, students, lovers and fools.
They don't take life too seriously;
   they travel light.
They leave no forwarding address;
   they ask for nothing in return.
They are hard to find when your eyes are
   closed but they are everywhere you look,
   when you choose to see.

Your Ten Cents Worth

A father and his son go to church. When services are over and they leave the church, Dad is complaining – the sermon was too long, the preacher was boring,

And the choir sang off-key.

Finally, the little boy said, "Daddy, I thought it was pretty good for just a dime."

Inner Peace—It's Catching

Folks almost everywhere have been exposed to inner peace, and they love it. Watch for these symptoms:

- A tendency to think and act spontaneously rather than on fears based on past experiences.
- An unmistakable ability to enjoy each moment.
- A loss of interest in judging other people.
- A loss of interest in interpreting the actions of others.
- A loss of interest in conflict.
- A loss of the ability to worry.

- Frequent, overwhelming episodes of appreciation.
- Contented feelings of being connected to others and nature.
- Frequent attacks of smiling.
- An increasing tendency to let things happen rather than make them happen.
- An increased susceptibility to the love offered by others as well as the uncontrollable urge to pass it on.

He Will Cover You with His Feathers

Forest rangers seeking to assess the damage caused several years ago by forest fires in Yellowstone Park accidentally came upon vivid testimony to God's promise of safety as described in Psalm 91:4: "He will cover you with his feathers, and under his wings you will find refuge; his faithfulness will be your shield and rampart."

One ranger found a bird literally petrified in ashes, perched on the ground at the base of a tree. Somewhat sickened by the sight, he knocked over the bird with a stick.

When it struck the bird, three tiny chicks scurried out from under their dead mother's wings.

The loving mother bird, keenly aware of the impending disaster, had carried her offspring to the base of the tree and had gathered them under her wings, instinctively knowing that the toxic smoke would rise. She could have flown to safety but had refused to abandon her babies. When the blaze arrived and the heat singed her small body, she remained steadfast.

Because she had been willing to die, her babies under the cover of her wings would live.

You Can't Out-Give God

A teenager was sitting in church, and when the collection plate was passed around, he quickly pulled a dollar bill from his pocket and dropped it in.

Just then, the person behind him tapped him on the shoulder and handed him a $20 bill. The boy smiled, placed the $20 in the plate and passed it on, admiring the man for being so generous.

Then the boy felt another tap from behind and heard another whisper "Son," the man said, "that was your $20 bill that had fallen out of your pocket."

Gotcha

It was a beautiful Sunday morning, and as a pastor was preparing for his message his eyes kept being drawn to the window where he could see the sun shining brightly outside. He started thinking, "What a great day to play golf."

So he called the elder in charge of the worship and told him that he was not feeling well and would not be able to preach that morning. When he got to the golf course, he began playing very well and proceeded to get one hole-in-one after another, ending with a perfect game.

As the pastor was finishing his round, Gabriel asked the Lord why he had helped the minister get a perfect game when he should have been at church. The Lord replied, "Who's he going to tell?"

Could You Be a Leader?

A leader is always full of praise.

A leader learns to use the phrases "thank you" and "please" on the way to the top.

A leader is always growing.

A leader is possessed with his dreams.

A leader launches forth before success is certain.

A leader is not afraid of confrontation.

Leaders talk about their own mistakes before talking about someone else's mistakes.

A leader is a person of honesty and integrity.

A leader has a good name.

A leader makes others better.

A leader is quick to praise and encourage the smallest amount of improvement.

A leader is genuinely interested in others.

A leader looks for opportunities to find someone doing something right.

Leaders take others up with them.

Leader respond to their own failures and acknowledge them before others have to discover and reveal them.

Leaders never allow murmuring—from themselves or others.

Leaders are specific in what they expect.

Leaders hold accountable those who work with them.

A leader does what is right rather than what is popular.

A leader is a servant.

The Guys in the Back

Six-year-old Tim and his three-year-old brother
Matthew were sitting together in church. Matthew
giggled, sang and talked out loud. Finally, his big
brother had heard enough. "You're not supposed to
talk out loud in church," he said.

"Why, who's going to stop me?" Matthew asked.

Tim pointed to the back of the church and said,
"See those two men standing by the door? They're
hushers."

This Thing Eats Nuts

Youth Pastor Jim was asked to give the children's message during church, so he decided to present an object lesson on how squirrels work so hard preparing for winter. He gathered the children around him and began.

"I want to describe something," Pastor Jim explained, "and I want you to raise your hand when you know what it is." The children nodded eagerly.

"This thing lives in trees," he paused. "And eats nuts." No hands went up.

"And it is gray," he paused again. "And it has a long bushy tail." The children were looking at each other, but still no hands raised.

"And it jumps from branch to branch and chatters and flips its tail when it is excited.

Finally one little boy tentatively raised his hand. Pastor Tim breathed a sigh of relief and called on him.

"Well," said the boy, "I know the answer must be Jesus...but it sure sounds like a squirrel to me."

Section III

Touched
by an
E-mail

Tears & Laughter When God Speaks

I Made You

Past the seeker as he prayed came the crippled and the beggar and the beaten.

And seeing them, he cried, "Great God, how is it that a loving Creator can see such things and yet do nothing about them?"

But God said, "I did do something.

I made you."

Please, Just Wait

Desperately, helplessly, longingly, I cried,
and quietly, patiently, God replied.
I had pled and had wept for a clue to my fate,
yet the Master just said, "Child, you must wait."

Wait? You say, wait, was my indignant reply.
Lord, I need answers. I need to know why.
Is your hand so short? Have you not heard?
By faith, I have asked, I am claiming your
Word.

My future and all to which I can relate
Now hangs in the balance. And you tell me to
"wait."
I need a "yes," a go-ahead sign,

Or even a "no" to which I resign.
Besides Lord, you promised that if we believe
we need but to ask, and we shall receive.
So Lord, I've been asking. This is my cry.
I'm weary of asking. I need a reply.

Then quietly, softly, I learned of my fate.
The Master replied, "My child, please just wait."

So I slumped in my chair, defeated and taut,
and grumbled to God, "OK, I am waiting, but
for what?"
He then seemed to kneel, His eyes wept with
mine, and tenderly said, "I could give you a
sign."

I could shake the heavens, darken the sun,
I could raise the dead and cause the mountains
to run.

All you seek, I could give. And then pleased you
would be?
You would have what you wanted, but you
wouldn't know me.

You'd not know the depth of my love, my dear
saint;
You'd not know the power I give to the faint;
You'd not learn to see through the clouds of
despair, that you need to trust, trusting simply,
"I'm here."

You'd not know the joy of resting in me,
when darkness and silence are all you can see;
You'd not experience all of my love,
when the peace of my Spirit descends like a
dove.

Oh, you'd know that I give, and I save . . . for a
start, but you'd miss the real joy of the depths
of my heart.
You'd miss the glow of my comfort through the
night and the faith that I give when you walk
without sight.

There's a depth far beyond getting what you
ask; the depth of my grace, getting what lasts.
You'd not know, should your pain quickly flee,
what it means when I say, "My grace is
sufficient for thee."

You'd have your dreams for your loved ones,
that's true,
But you'd miss, oh you'd miss, what I'm doing
in you.
So be silent, my child, in time you will see

that my greatest gift is to get to know me.
And though oft my answers seem terribly late,
my most precious answer still is, "Just wait."

Why Am I Failing?

A man was sleeping in his cabin one night when suddenly his room was filled with light and the Savior appeared. The Lord told the man he had work for him to do, and showed him a large rock in front of his cabin.

The Lord explained that the man was to push against the rock with all his might.

This the man did, day after day. For many years he toiled from sun to sundown, his shoulders set squarely against the cold, massive surface of the unmoving rock, pushing with all his might. Each night the man returned to his cabin sore and worn out, feeling that his whole day had been spent in vain. Seeing that the man was showing signs of discouragement, Satan decided to enter the picture by placing doubts into the man's weary mind: "You have been pushing against the rock for a long time and it hasn't budged. Why kill yourself over this? You are never going to move it." He gave the man the impression that the task was impossible and that he was a failure. Discouraged and disheartened, the man thought, "Why kill myself? I'll just put in my time, giving the minimum effort and that will be good enough."

And that was what he planned to do until one day he decided to make it a matter of prayer and take his troubled thoughts to the Lord. "Lord," he said, "I have labored long and hard in your service, putting all my strength to do what you have asked. Yet, after all this time, I have not even budged that rock one inch. What's wrong? Why am I failing?"

The Lord responded compassionately, "My friend, when I asked you to serve me and you accepted, I told you that your task was to push against the rock with all your strength, which you have done.

Never once did I mention to you that I expected you to move it. Your task was to push.

"And now you come to me with your strength spent, thinking that you have failed. But is that really so? Look at yourself. Your arms are strong, your back is muscular, and your legs are have become massive and hard. Through opposition, you have grown much and your abilities now surpass what you used to have.

Yet you haven't moved the rock. But your calling was to be obedient and to push and to exercise your faith and trust in My wisdom. This you have done. "I, my friend, will now move the rock."

Letting Go

As children bring their broken toys,
  with tears for us to mend.
I brought my broken dreams to God,
  because He is my friend.

But then instead of leaving Him
  in peace to work alone,
I hung around and tried to help,
  with ways that were my own.

At last I snatched them back again
  and cried, "How can you be so slow?"
"My child," He said, "What could I do?
  You never did let go."

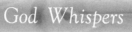

God Whispers

The little things
The little moments?
They aren't little.

Dear Friend

As you got up this morning I watched you and hoped you would talk to me even if it was just a few words, asking my opinion or thanking me for something good that happened in your life. But I noticed you were too busy trying to find the right outfit to wear to work.

I waited again. When you ran around the house getting ready, I knew there would be a few minutes for you to stop and say hello, but you were too busy. At one point you had to wait fifteen minutes with nothing to do except sit in a chair. Then I saw you spring to your feet. I thought you wanted to talk to me, but you ran to the phone and called a friend to get the latest gossip.

I watched as you went to work and I waited patiently all day long. With all your activities I guess you were too busy to say anything to me. I noticed that before lunch you looked around, maybe you felt embarrassed to talk to me and that is why you didn't bow your head. You glanced three or four tables over and noticed some of your friends talking to me briefly before they ate, but you didn't. That's okay. There is still more time left, and I have hope that you will talk to me even yet.

You went home and it seems as if you had lots of things to do. After a few of them were done you turned on the TV. I don't know if I like TV or not, just about anything goes there and you spend a lot of time each day in front of it not thinking about anything but the show. I waited patiently again as you watched TV and ate your meal, but again you didn't talk to me. As you did your paperwork I waited again while you did what you had to do.

At bedtime I guess you felt too tired. After you said goodnight to your family you plopped into bed and fell asleep in no time. That's okay because you may not realize that I am always there for you. I've got patience – more than you will ever know. I even want to teach you how to be patient with others as well. Because I love you so much, a long time ago I left a wonderful place called Heaven and came to Earth. I gave it up so that I could be ridiculed. And I even died so you wouldn't have to take my place.

I love you so much that I wait everyday for a nod, a prayer, a thought or a heartfelt thank you. It is hard to have a one-sided conversation.

Well, you are about to wake up and once again I will wait with nothing but love for you, hoping that today you will give me some time. Have a nice day.

Your friend,
Jesus Christ

God Said "No"

I asked God to take away my pride.
God said "No."
It is not for me to take away, but for you to give
it up.
I asked God to make my handicapped child
whole.
God said "No."
Her spirit was whole, her body was only
temporary.
I asked God to grant me patience.
God said "No."
Patience is a by-product of tribulations; it isn't
granted, it is earned.
I asked God to give me happiness.
God said "No."

I give you blessings, happiness is up to you.

I asked God to spare me pain.

God said "No."

Suffering draws you apart from worldly cares
and brings you closer to me.

I asked God to make my spirit grow.

God said "No."

You must grow on your own, but I will prune
you to make you fruitful.

I asked for all things that I might enjoy life.

God said "No."

I will give you life so that you may enjoy all
things.

I asked God to help me love others as much as
he love me.

God said, "Ahhh, finally you have the idea,"

Top Ten Reasons God Created Eve

Number 10: God worried that Adam would always be lost in the garden because men hate to ask directions.

Number 9: God knew that Adam would one day need someone to hand him the TV remote. Men don't want to see what "on" television; they want to see "what else is on."

Number 8: God knew that Adam would never buy a new fig leaf when he needed one and that Eve would have to do it for him.

Number 7: God knew that Adam would need someone to make his doctor's appointments for him.

Number 6: God knew that Adam would never remember to put the garbage out.

Number 5: God knew that if the world was to be populated that Adam could never handle the childbearing.

Number 4: As keeper of the garden, Adam would never remember where he put his tools.

Number 3: The scripture account of creation indicates Adam needed someone to blame his troubles on when God caught him hiding in the garden.

Number 2: As the Bible says, "It is not good for man to be alone."

And the Number 1 reason why God created Eve: When God finished the creation of Adam, He stepped back, scratched His head, and said, "I can do better than that."

It's In The Book

We say: It's impossible"

God says: All things are possible (Luke 18:27)

We say: "I'm too tired"

God says: I will give you rest (Matthew 11:28-30)

We say: "Nobody really loves me"

God says: I love you (John 3:16 and John 13:34)

We say: "I can't go on"

God says: My grace is sufficient
(II Corinthians 12:9 and Psalm 91:15)

We say: "I can't figure things out"

God says: I will direct your steps
(Proverbs 3:5-6)

We say: "I can't do it"
God says: You can do all things (Philippians 4:13)
We say: "I'm not able"
God says: I am able (II Corinthians 9:8)
We say: "It's not worth it"
God says: It will be worth it (Romans 8:28)
We say: "I can't forgive myself"
God says: I forgive you (I John 1:9 and Romans 8:1)
We say: "I can't manage"
God says: I will supply all your needs (Philippians 4:19)
We say: "I'm afraid"
God says: I have not given you a spirit of fear (II Timothy 1:7)
We say: "I'm always worried and frustrated"
God says: Cast all your worries on me (I Peter 5:7)

We say: "I don't have enough faith"
God says: I've given everyone a measure of
faith (Romans 12:3)
We say: "I'm not smart enough"
God says: I give you wisdom (I Corinthians
1:30)
We say: "I feel all alone"
And God says: I will never leave you or forsake
you (Hebrews 13:5)

The Angel In Your Life

Once upon a time there was a child ready to be born. So one day she asked God, "They tell me you are sending me to earth tomorrow but how am I going to live there being so small and helpless?"

God replied, "Among the many angels, I chose one for you. She will be waiting for you and will take care of you."

"But tell me, here in Heaven, I don't do anything else but sing and smile. That's enough for me to be happy."

God said, "Your angel will sing for you and will also smile for you every day. And you will feel your angel's love and be happy."

"And how am I going to be able to understand when people talk to me if I don't know the language that men talk?"

"Your angel will tell you the most beautiful and sweet words you will ever hear, and with much patience and care, your angel will teach you how to speak."

"And what am I going to do when I want to talk to you?"

God said, "Your angel will place your hands together and will teach you how to pray."

"I've heard that on earth there are bad people. Who will protect me?"

"Your angel will defend you even if it means risking its life."

"But I will always be sad because I will not see you anymore."

"Your angel will always talk to you about me and will teach you the way for you to come back to me, even though I will always be next to you."

At the moment there was much peace in Heaven, but voices from earth could already be heard, and the child in a hurry asked softly,

"Oh God, if I am about to leave now, please tell me my angel's name."

God silenced all fear when He said, "Your angel's name is of no importance. You will simply call her 'Mommy'."

A Room Filled with Crosses

The young man was at the end of his rope. Seeing no way out, he dropped to his knees in prayer.

"Lord, I can't go on," he said. "I have too heavy a cross to bear."

The Lord replied, "My son, if you can't bear its weight, just place your cross inside this room. Then, open that other door and pick out any cross you wish."

The man was filled with relief. "Thank you, Lord," he sighed, and he did as he was told. Upon entering the other door, he saw many crosses, some so large the tops were not visible. Then he spotted a tiny cross leaning against a far wall. "I'd like that one, Lord," he whispered.

And the Lord replied, "My son, that is the cross you just brought in."

The young man had just been taught that when life's problems seem overwhelming, he should look around and see the problems of others.

He probably will find—as we all would—that he is far more fortunate than he ever imagined.

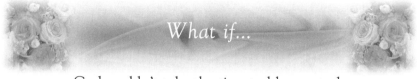

What if...

God couldn't take the time to bless us today, because we couldn't take the time to thank Him yesterday?

What if...
God decided to stop leading us tomorrow, because we didn't follow Him today?

What if...
God didn't walk with us today, because we failed to recognize it as His day?

What if...
We never saw another flower bloom, because we grumbled when God sent the rain?

What if...

God stopped loving and caring for us because we failed to love and care for others?

What if...

God took away the Bible tomorrow, because we wouldn't read it today?

What if...

God took away His message, because we failed to listen to His messenger?

What if...

God didn't send His only begotten Son, because He wanted us to be prepared to pay the price of sin?

What if...

The door to the church was closed,   because we did not open the door to our hearts?

What if...

God would not hear us today, because we would not listen to Him yesterday?

What if...

God answered our prayers the way we answer His call to service?

What if...

God met our needs the way we give Him our lives?

Somebody

Somebody is very proud of you.

Somebody is thinking of you.

Somebody cares about you.

Somebody misses you.

Somebody wants to talk with you.

Somebody hopes you are not in trouble.

Somebody is thankful for your support.

Somebody wants to hold your hand.

Somebody wants you to be happy.

Somebody wants you to find them.

Somebody wants to hug you.

Somebody thinks you are a gift from God.

Somebody admires your strength.

Somebody wants to protect you.

Somebody can't wait to see you.

Somebody treasures your spirit.

Somebody is glad you are their friend.

Somebody trusts you.

Somebody wants to share your dreams.

Somebody wants to get to know you better.

Somebody is alive because of you.

Somebody wants you to know they are there for
you.

Somebody needs you to have faith in them.

Somebody hears a song that reminds them of
you.

Somebody—maybe several somebodies—needs
to hear from you today.

Section IV

Touched by an E-mail

Tears & Laughter at Home

Thank God for Unmade Beds

Thank you, God, for all I have to do today.
Thanks, God, for this sink of dirty dishes;
It shows we have plenty to eat.
Thanks, God, for this pile of dirty, smelly
laundry;
It shows we have plenty of clothes to wear.
Thanks, God, for those unmade beds in there;
they were warm and so comfortable last night,
and I know there are many who have no beds.
Thank you, God, for this bathroom, complete
with the spattered mirror, all the soggy, grimy
towels and the dirty commode.
They are so convenient.
Thanks, God, for this finger-smudged
refrigerator that needs defrosting.

It is full of cold drinks and enough leftovers for
two or three meals.
Thanks, God, for this oven
that absolutely must be cleaned today.
It has baked so many things over the years.
The whole family is grateful for the grass that
needs mowing, the lawn that will need raking.
We all enjoy the yard.
Thanks, God, even for that slamming screen
door.
My kids are healthy and able to run and play.
Lord, the presence of all these chores awaiting
me says you have richly blessed my family.
I shall do them all cheerfully;
And I shall do them gratefully.

Instructions for Life

1. Give people more than they expect and do it cheerfully.

2. Don't believe all you hear, spend all you have, or sleep all you want.

3. When you lose, don't lose the lesson.

4. Smile when you pick up the phone. The caller will hear it in your voice.

5. Talk slowly, but think quickly.

6. Don't judge people by their relatives.

7. Never interrupt when you are being flattered.

8. Remember that silence is sometimes the best answer.

9. Remember that not getting what you want is sometimes a stroke of luck.

10. When someone asks you a question you don't want to answer, smile and ask, "Why do you want to know?"

He's Got it all Figured Out

One summer afternoon, a mom was simply exasperated with her young son's antics. She snapped at him, saying, ""How do you ever expect to get into heaven when you act this way?"

"Well," fidgeted little Jimmy after some thought, "I'll run in and out and keep slamming the door until they say 'Come in or stay out' and then I'll go in."

What Did You Do Today?

One day a father comes home from work to find total mayhem in the house. The kids were outside playing in the mud and muck, still in their pajamas. There were empty food boxes and wrappers all around. As he proceeded into the house, he found an even bigger mess. Dirty dishes covered the kitchen counter, dog food was spilled on the floor and there was a small pile of sand by the back door. The family room was strewn with toys and various items of clothing. And a lamp had been knocked over.

He headed up the stairs, stepping over toys, to look for his wife. He was becoming worried that she may be ill, or that something had happened to her. He found her in the bedroom, still in bed with her nightgown on, reading a book. She looked up at him and smiled, and asked him how his day went. He looked at her bewildered and asked, "What happened here today?"

She smiled again and answered, "You know everyday when you come home from work and ask me what I did today?"

"Yes," he said.

"Well, today I didn't do it," she answered.

Yesterday is Gone

There are two days in every week about which we need not worry.

One of these days is yesterday with its mistakes and cares, its faults and blunders, its aches and pains. Yesterday has passed forever beyond our control. All the money in the world cannot bring back yesterday. We cannot undo a single act we performed. We cannot erase a single word we said. Yesterday is gone.

The other day we should not worry about is tomorrow, with its possible adversities, its burdens, its large promise and poor performance. Tomorrow is beyond our immediate control. Tomorrow's sun will rise, whether in splendor or behind a mask of clouds. But it will rise. Until it does we have no stake in tomorrow for it is as yet unborn.

This leaves only one day: today. Any person can fight the battles of just one day. It is when you add the burdens of two awful eternities – yesterday and tomorrow – that we break down.

It is not necessarily the experience of today that disturbs one's peace of mind.

It is often the bitterness for something that has happened yesterday and the dread of what tomorrow may bring.

Life is like Basketball

You will always miss 100 percent of
the shots you don't take.

A Father

A father is a person who is forced to endure childbirth without an anesthetic. He growls when he feels good and laughs very loud when he is scared half to death.

A father never feels entirely worthy of the worship in a child's eyes. He is never quite the hero his daughter thinks...never quite the man his son believes him to be. And this worries him sometimes, so he works too hard to try to smooth the rough places in the road of those of his own who follow him.

A father is a person who goes to war sometimes, but he would rather run the other way except that war is part of his only important job in life—making the world better for his child than it has been for him.

Fathers grow older faster than other people because they, in other wars, have to stand at the train station and wave goodbye to the uniform that climbs on board.

And while mothers cry where it shows, fathers stand and beam...outside, and die inside.

Fathers are men who give daughters away to other men, who aren't nearly good enough, so that they can have children that are smarter than anybody's.

Paid In Full

A young man was getting ready to graduate from college, and he was expecting a beautiful new sports car for a gift. He knew his dad could afford it, and he had told him that's what he wanted.

On the morning of graduation, the young man's father called him into his private study. His father told him how proud he was to have such a fine son, and told him how much he loved him. He handed his son a beautifully wrapped box.

Curious and somewhat disappointed, the young man opened the box and found a lovely, leather-bound Bible with his name embossed in gold. Angry, he raised his voice to his father and said, "with all your money you give me a Bible?" and he stormed from the house.

Many years passed and the young man was successful in business, had a wonderful home and family. He realized his father was very old and he thought perhaps he should go to see him. He had not seen his father since that graduation day. Before he could make arrangements, he received notice that his father had died and willed him all of his possessions. He needed to come home immediately to take care of things.

When he arrived at his father's house, sadness and regret suddenly filled his heart. He began to search through his father's papers and saw the still new Bible, just as he had left it years ago. With tears, he opened the Bible and began to turn the pages. His father had carefully underlined a verse, Matthew 7:11. "And if ye, being evil, know how to give good gifts to your children, how much more shall your Heavenly Father which is in Heaven, give to those who ask him?"

As he read those words, a car key dropped from the back of the Bible. It had a tag with the dealer's name, the same dealer who had the sports car he had desired. On the tag was the date of his graduation, and the words, "Paid in Full."

The Answer is "Nothing"

What is greater than God,
More evil than the devil,
The poor have it,
The rich need it,
And if you eat it, you'll die?

What is a Cat? What is a Dog?

What is a cat?

- Cats do what they want.
- They rarely listen to you.
- They're totally unpredictable.
- They whine when they are not happy.
- When you want to play, they want to be alone.
- When you want to be alone, they want to play.
- They expect you to cater to their every whim.
- They're moody.
- They leave hair everywhere.
- They drive you nuts and cost an arm and a leg.

Conclusion: They're tiny little women in fur coats.

What is a dog?

- Dogs lie around all day, sprawled on the most comfortable piece of furniture in the house.
- They can hear a package of food opening half a block away, but don't hear you when you're in the same room.
- They can look dumb and lovable all at the same time.
- They growl when they are not happy.
- When you want to play, they want to be alone.
- When you want to be alone, they want to play.

- They are great at begging.
- They will love you forever if you rub their tummies.
- They leave their toys everywhere.
- They do disgusting things with their mouths and then try to give you a kiss.

Conclusion: They're little men in fur coats.

Don't Throw it Away

Have you made someone happy, or made
someone sad, What have you done with the day
that you had.
God gave it to you to do just as you would.
Did you do what was wicked or do what was
good?
Did you hand out a smile or just give a frown,
Did you list someone up, or push someone
down?
Did you lighten some load or some progress
impede,
Did you look for a rose or just gather a weed?
What did you do with your beautiful day,
God gave it to you, did you throw it away?

I've Got A Favor To Ask

A young soldier just returning from the battlefields of Vietnam called his parents as soon as he reached the United States.

"Mom and Dad, I'm coming home, but I've got a favor to ask. I have a friend I'd like to bring with me." "Sure," they replied, "we'd love to meet him."

"There's something you should know," the son continued. "He was badly hurt in the fighting. He stepped on a land mine and lost and arm and a leg. He has nowhere else to go, and I want him to come live with us."

"I'm sorry to hear that, son," his parents said. "Maybe we can help him find somewhere to live."

"No, Mom and Dad, I want him to live with us," the son went on.

"Son," said the father, "you don't know what you're asking. Someone with such a handicap would be a terrible burden on us. We have our own lives to live, and we can't let something like this interfere. I think you should just come home and forget about your friend."

At that point, the son hung up the phone. And his parents heard nothing more from him.

A few days later, the parents received a call from the police. Their son had died after jumping from a tall building. The parents were grief-stricken as they traveled to the morgue to identify the body.

They recognized him, but to their horror they also discovered something they didn't know. Their son had only one arm and one leg.

Almost As Good

If you can start the day without caffeine,

If you can get going without pep pills,

If you can always be cheerful, ignoring aches
and pains,

If you can resist complaining and boring people
with your troubles,

If you can eat the same food everyday and be
grateful for it,

If you can understand when your loved ones are
too busy to give you any time,

If you can overlook it when those you love take
it out on you when, through no fault of
yours, something goes wrong,

If you can take criticism and blame without
resentment,

136

If you can ignore a friend's limited education
and never correct him,
If you can resist treating a rich friend better
than a poor friend,
If you can face the world without lies and
deceit,
If you can conquer tension without medical
help.
If you can relax without liquor,
If you can sleep without the aid of drugs,
If you can say honestly that deep in your heart
you have no prejudice against creed, color,
religion or politics,
Then, my friend, you are almost as good as
your dog.

A Lifetime of Learning

Age 6:

I've learned that I like my teacher because she cries when we sing "Silent Night."

Age 7:

I've learned that you can't hide a piece of broccoli in a glass of milk.

Age 9:

I've learned that when I wave to people in the country, they stop what they're doing and wave back.

Age 13:

I've learned that just when I get my room the way I like it, Mom makes me clean it.

Age 14:

I've learned that if you want to cheer yourself up, you should try cheering someone else up.

Age 15:

I've learned that although it's hard to admit it, I'm secretly glad my parents are strict with me.

Age 24:

I've learned that silent company is often more healing than words of advice.

Age 26:

I've learned that brushing my child's hair is one of life's pleasures.

Age 29:

I've learned that wherever I go, the world's worst drivers have followed me there.

Age 39:

I've learned that if someone says something unkind about me, I must live so that no one will believe it.

Age 41:

I've learned that there are people who love you dearly but just don't know how to show it.

Age 44:

I've learned that you can make someone's day by simply sending them a little card.

Age 46:

I've learned that the greater a person's sense of guilt, the greater his need to cast blame on others.

Age 47:

I've learned that children and grandparents are natural allies.

Age 49:

I've learned that singing Amazing Grace can lift my spirits for hours.

Age 52:

I've learned that you can tell a lot about a man by the way he handles three things: a rainy day, lost luggage, and tangled Christmas tree lights.

Age 53:

I've learned that regardless of your relationship with your parents, you miss them terribly after they die.

Age 58:

I've learned that making a living is not the same thing as making a life.

Age 62:

I've learned that making a life sometimes gives you a second chance.

Age 64:

I've learned that you shouldn't go through life with a catcher's mitt on both hands. You need to be able to throw something back.

Age 65:

I've learned that if you pursue happiness it will elude you. But if you focus on your family, the needs of others, your work, always doing the very best you can, happiness will find you.

Age 68:

I've learned that whenever I do something with kindness, I usually make the right decision.

Age 72:

I've learned that everyone can use a prayer.

Age 73: I've learned that it pays to believe in miracles. And to tell the truth, I've seen several.

Age 82:

I've learned that even when I have pains, I don't have to be one.

Age 85:

I've learned that every day you should reach out and touch someone. People love that human touch – holding hands, a warm hug, or just a friendly pat on the back.

Age 92:

I've learned that I still have a lot to learn.

How to be a Good Neighbor

A man left his house for church one Sunday just as his neighbor was loading his golf clubs into his car. "Henry," the neighbor called, "come play golf with me today."

Henry answered firmly, "I always go to church on the Lord's Day."

After a pause, the golfer said, "You know, Henry, I've often wondered about your church and I really admire your faithfulness. But I've invited you to play golf with me seven or eight times, and you've never once invited me to go to church with you."

You Have a Choice

Jerry is the kind of guy who is always in a good mood. You don't know how he does it. He always has something positive to say. When someone would ask him how he was doing, he would reply, "If I were any better, I would be twins."

He was a unique restaurant manager because he had several waiters who followed him from restaurant to restaurant. They loved his attitude. He was a motivator. If an employee was having a bad day, Jerry was there telling them to look on the positive side.

When folks questioned Jerry about this attitude, Jerry would tell them, "Each morning I wake up and say to myself, Jerry, you have two choices today. You can choose to be in a good mood or you can choose to be in a bad mood. I always choose to be in a good mood. Each time something bad happens, I can choose to be a victim or I can choose to learn from it. So I choose to learn. Every time someone comes to me complaining, I can choose to accept their complaining or I can point out the positive side of life. I choose the positive side.

People tell Jerry that doing this is not easy. But he says, "Yes, it is. Life is all abut choices. When you cut away the junk, every situation presents a choice. You choose how you react to situations. You choose how people will affect your mood. You chose to be in a good mood or bad mood. It's your choice how you live life."

One day Jerry had let the back door to his restaurant open and he was held up at gunpoint by three armed robbers. During the robbery, Jerry was shot and seriously wounded. This is how he tells that story.

"The first thing that went through my mind,"

Jerry says, "was that I should have locked the back door. Then as I lay wounded on the floor, I remembered that I had two choices: I could choose to live or choose to die. I chose to live.

"The paramedics were great," he remembers. "They kept telling me I was going to be fine. But when they wheeled me into the emergency room and I saw the expressions on the faces of the doctors and nurses, I really got scared. In their eyes I read 'he's a dead man'. I knew I had to take action."

When the nurse asked Jerry if he was allergic to anything, he said, "Yes, bullets."

Over their laughter, Jerry kept telling them, "I choose to live. Operate as if I'm alive, not dead."

Jerry lives because of the skill of the doctors and his amazing attitude. Every day we can make the same kind of choices Jerry does. We can choose to live fully or we can choose not to.

Consult Not Your Fears

Consult not your fears
but your hopes and your dreams.

Think not about your frustrations,
 but about your unfulfilled potential.

Concern yourself
not with what you tried and failed in,
but with what is still possible
for you to do.

Journal Entry

"I am the hot tears on a friend's face who can feel someone's pain as their own.

I am an impatient mother who loves her children so much and is afraid that they really won't know how deep that love is.

I am the denier of the Holy Spirit who, though I rarely listen, continues to prompt me.

I am a survivor.

I am an old friend of pain.

I am a newer friend to happiness, peace and joy.

I am learning that joy isn't pain-free, and happiness isn't joy, and peace can be in the presence of chaos.

And Then Mom Said

A woman invited some people to dinner. At the table, she turned to her six-year-old daughter and asked her to say the blessing. "I wouldn't know what to say," the little girl replied. "Just say what you hear mommy say," the mother said.

The little girl bowed her head and said, "Dear Lord, why on earth did I invite all these people to dinner?"

Section V

Touched by an E-mail

Tears and Laughter While Praying

Please Give Me

Dear Lord, please give me
A few friends who understand me and remain
   my friends;
A work to do which has real value,
   without which the world would be poorer;
A mind unafraid to travel, even though the
   trail be not blazed;
An understanding heart;
A sense of humor;
Time for quiet, silent meditation;
A feeling of the presence of God;
The patience to wait for the coming of these
   things, with the wisdom to recognize them
   when they come.

A Little Mouse Shall Lead Them

A mother was teaching her three-year-old daughter The Lord's Prayer. For several evenings at bedtime, little Linda repeated it after her mother.

One night, Linda told her mom she was ready to say the prayer alone. The mother listened with pride as she carefully enunciated each word.. right up to the end.

"Lead us not into temptation but deliver us some e-mail. Amen."

Seven Days without Prayer Makes One Weak

Bicycle around your neighborhood, stopping by the churches you see. In many cases you will quickly become aware that some of the most clever writing being done today is by the folks who compose one-letter-at-a-time invitations on church signs. Here are some examples:

God is always on time.
Give the devil and inch, and he'll become your
   ruler.
By perseverance, the snails reached the ark.
Difficulties in life can make us better or bitter.
Prayer is the oil that takes the friction out of
   life.

The wages of sin will not be lowered.

The devil's not afraid of a Bible with dust on it.

Many people hope to be elected to Heaven who are not even running for office.

A person never stands as tall as when kneeling before God.

God's 911 Numbers

When in sorrow, call John 14.

If you want to be fruitful, call John 15.

When you have sinned, call Psalm 51

When you worry, call Matthew 6:19-34

When you are in danger, call Psalm 91

When God seems far away, call Psalm 139.

When your faith needs stirring, call Hebrews 11.

When you are lonely and fearful, call Psalm 23.

When you grow bitter and critical, call
I Corinthians 13.

For Paul's secret to happiness, call Colossians
3:12-17.

For an idea of Christianity, call 1 Corinthians
5:15-19.

When you feel down and out, call Romans
8:31-39.

When you want peace and rest, call Matthew
11:25-30.

When the world seems bigger than God, call
Psalm 90.

When you want Christian assurance, call
Romans 8:1-30.

When you leave home for labor or travel, call
Psalm 121.

When your prayers grow narrow or selfish, call
Psalm 67.

When you want courage for a task, call
Joshua 1.

If you are depressed, call Psalm 27.

If your pocketbook is empty, call Psalm 37.

If you're losing confidence in people, call
I Corinthians 13.

If people seem unkind, call John 15.

If discouraged about your work, call Psalm 126.

If you find the world small and yourself great, call Psalm 19.

All lines are open 24 hours a day.

We Pray For You

Enough happiness to keep you sweet

Enough trials to keep you strong

Enough sorrow to keep you human

Enough hope to keep you happy

Enough failure to keep you humble

Enough success to keep you eager

Enough friends to give you comfort

Enough wealth to meet your needs

Enough enthusiasm to look forward

Enough faith to banish depression

Enough determination to make each day better than yesterday

Slow Me Down Lord

Slow me down Lord, ease the pounding of my heart by the quieting of my mind. Steady my pace with the vision of the eternal reach of time.

Give me, amid the confusion of the day, the calmness of the everlasting hills. Break the tensions of my nerves and muscles with the soothing music of the singing streams that still live in my memory.

Help me to know the magical restoring power of sleep, teach me the art of taking minute vacations, of slowing down to look at a flower, to chat with a friend, to pat a dog, to answer a child's question or to read a few lines from a good book.

Remind me each day of the fable of the hare and the tortoise that I may know that the race is not always to the swift, that there is more to life than just increasing its speed.

Let me look upward into the branches of a towering oak and know that it grew slowly and well from a tiny acorn.

Slow me down Lord and inspire me to send my roots, deep into the soil of life's enduring values, that I may grow more surely towards the stars.

He Tried to Weigh A Prayer

A tired looking woman came into a grocery store and asked for enough food to make a dinner for her children.

The grocer asked her what she could spend, and the frail woman answered, "I have nothing to offer but a little prayer."

The storekeeper was not very sentimental or religious, so he said somewhat mockingly, "Write it on paper, and I'll weigh it." So she did.

The grocer placed the prayer on the weight side of his old-fashioned scales. Then he began piling food on the other side; but to his amazement, the scale would not go down. He finally became flustered and gave the woman a large bag of food.

The grocer never saw the woman again, but today he treasures the slip of paper upon which the woman's prayer had been written: "Please, Lord, give us this day our daily bread."

Eat Your Greens

Six-year-old Erica was asked to say grace before Thanksgiving dinner. The family members bowed their heads in expectation.

She began the prayer thanking God for all her friends, naming them one by one. Then she thanked God for Mommy, Daddy, Grandma, all her aunts and uncles and cousins.

Then she began to thank God for the food. She gave thanks for the turkey, the dressing, the fruit salad, the cranberry sauce, the pies, the cakes and even the whipped cream.

Then she paused, and everyone waited and waited. After a long silence, the young girl looked up at her mother and asked, "If I thank God for the broccoli, won't He know that I'm lying?"

The Stone Cutter

There was once a stone cutter who was dissatisfied with himself and with his position in life.

One day he passed a wealthy merchant's house. Through the open gateway, he saw many fine possessions and important visitors. "How powerful that merchant must be!" thought the stone cutter. He became very envious and wished that he could be like the merchant.

To his great surprise, he suddenly became the merchant, enjoying more luxuries and power than he had ever imagined, but envied and detested by those less wealthy than himself. Soon a high official passed by, carried in a sedan chair, accompanied by attendants and escorted by soldiers beating gongs. Everyone, no matter how wealthy, had to bow low before the procession. "How powerful that official is," he thought. "I wish that I could be a high official!"

Then he became a high official, carried everywhere in his embroidered sedan chair, feared and hated by the people all around. It was a hot summer day, so the official felt very uncomfortable in the sticky sedan chair. He looked up at the sun. It shone proudly in the sky, unaffected by his presence. "How powerful the sun is!" he thought. "I wish that I could be the sun!"

Then he became the sun, shining fiercely down on everyone, scorching the fields, cursed by the farmers and laborers. But a huge black cloud moved between him and the earth, so that his light could no longer shine on everything below. "How powerful the storm cloud is," he thought. "I wish that I could be a cloud!"

Then he became the cloud, flooding the fields and villages, shouted at by everyone. But soon he found that he was being pushed away by some great force, and he realized that it was the wind. "How powerful it is," he thought. "I wish I could be the wind!"

Then he became the wind, blowing tiles off the roofs of houses, uprooting trees, feared and hated by all below him. But after a while, he ran up against something that would not move, no matter how forcefully he blew against it – a huge towering rock. "How powerful that rock is!" he thought. "I wish that I could be a rock!"

Then he became the rock, more powerful than anything else on earth.

But as he stood there, he heard the sound of a hammer pounding a chisel into the hard surface and felt himself being changed. "What could be more powerful than I, the rock?" he thought.

He looked down and saw far below him the figure of a stone cutter.

He Sends The Very Best

A woman was at work when she received a phone call that her daughter was very sick with a fever. She left work and stopped by the pharmacy to get some medication for her daughter. Upon returning to her car she found that she had locked her keys in the car. She was in a hurry to get home to her sick daughter , and she didn't know what to do.

She called the babysitter and was told her daughter was getting worse.

The sitter suggested that the woman find a coat hanger and try to open the door. After looking around, she found an old rusty hanger that probably had been used by someone else for the same purpose. Then she looked at the hanger and said, "I don't know how to use this." So she bowed her head and asked God to send some help.

Within five minutes, and old car pulled up with a dirty bearded man who was wearing a greasy biker skull rag on his head. The woman thought, "Lord, this is what You sent to help me?"

But she was desperate, so she was very thankful. The man got out of his car and asked her if he could help. She said, "Yes, my daughter is very sick. I must get home, but I've locked my keys in the car. Please, can you use this hanger to unlock my car?"

He walked over to the car, and in less than one minute the car was opened. She hugged the man and through her tears she said, "Thank you so much. You are a very nice man."

The man replied, "Lady, I'm not a nice man. I just got out of prison today. I was in prison for car theft and have only been out for about an hour."

The woman hugged the man again and while sobbing cried out loud,

"Oh, thank you, God. You sent me a professional!"

Will We Have a Test?

Blessed are the poor in spirit, for theirs is the
kingdom of heaven

Blessed are the meek

Blessed are they who mourn

Blessed are the merciful

Blessed are they who thirst for justice

Blessed are you when persecuted

Blessed are you when you suffer

Be glad and rejoice, for your reward is great in
heaven..

Then Simon Peter said, "Do we have to write
this down?"

And Andrew said, "Are we supposed to know
this?"

And James said, "Will we have a test on it?"

173

And Philip said, "What if we don't know it?"

And Bartholomew said, "Do we have to turn this in?"

And John said, "The other disciples didn't have to learn this."

And Matthew said, "When do we get out of here?"

And Judas said, "What does this have to do with real life?"

Then one of the Pharisees present asked to see Jesus' lessons plans and inquired of Jesus his terminal objectives in the cognitive domain.

And Jesus wept...

Dear Lord

Please give me:
A few friends who understand me
    and remain my friends;
A work to do which has real value,
    without which the world would be poorer;
A mind unafraid to travel
    even though the trail be not blazed;
An understanding heart:
A sense of humor;
Time for quiet, silent meditation;
A feeling of the presence of God;
The patience to wait for the coming of these
    things, with the wisdom to recognize them
    when they come.
Amen.

Good Morning, God

You are ushering in another day,
Untouched and freshly new.
So here I come to ask you, God,
If you'll renew me, too.

Forgive the many errors
That I made yesterday.
And let me try again, dear God,
To walk closer in Thy way.

But Father, I am well aware
I can't make it on my own.
So take my hand and hold it tight,
For I cannot walk alone.

The Prayer of a Golden-Ager

God, grant me the senility
   to forget the people I never liked anyway,
The good fortune
   to run into the ones I do,
And the eyesight
   to tell the difference.

Faith's Reward

Faith is to believe what we do
    not see;
The reward of this faith is to
    see what we believe.

— St. Augustine

Someone Once Asked

"Why is it when we talk to God,
we are said to be praying?
And when God talks to us, we
are said to be schizophrenic.

179

But Don't Forget

Forget about the days when it's been cloudy, but don't forget your hours in the sun.

Forget about the times you've been defeated but don't forget the victories you have won.

Forget about the mistakes that you can't change now, but don't forget the lessons you have learned.

Forget about the misfortunes you've encountered, but don't forget the times your luck has turned.

Forget about the days when you've been lonely, but don't forget the friendly smiles you've seen.

Forget about the plans that didn't seem to work right, but don't forget to always have a dream.

More Precious Than Rubies

A woman was traveling in the mountains and found a precious stone lying in the middle of the road. The next day she met another traveler. He was hungry, and the woman opened her bag to share her food. But the hungry traveler saw the precious stone and asked the woman to give it to him. She did without hesitation, and the traveler left excited by his good fortune. But a few days later, he came back to the woman to return the stone.

"I've been thinking," he said. "I know how valuable the stone is, but I return it in the hope that you can give me something even more precious. Give me what you have within you that enabled you to give me the stone."

181

Love Them Anyway

People are unreasonable, illogical and self-
  centered.
Love them anyway.

If you do good, people will accuse you of selfish,
  ulterior motives.
Do good anyway.

If you are successful, you will win false friends
  and true enemies.
Succeed anyway.

The good you do today may be forgotten
  tomorrow.
Do good anyway.

Honesty and frankness make you vulnerable.
Be honest anyway.

The biggest person with the biggest ideas can be
    shot down by the smallest person with the
    smallest mind.
Think big anyway.

What you spend years building may be
    destroyed overnight.
Build anyway.

People really need help but may attack you if
    you help them.
Help people anyway.

Give the world the best you have and in some
    ways you may fail.
Give the world the best you have anyway.

And the Light Came On

William was a university student in training for the Summer Olympics some years ago. He was an excellent high diver.

He had a good friend who would speak with him for hours about the Lord and the path to eternal life. William had been reared in a home that had not attended any kind of church, so all that his friend told him held some fascination. William even began to ask questions about the forgiveness of sin.

Finally, the day came when the friend put the question to William. He asked him if he realized his own need for a Redeemer and if he was ready to trust Christ as his own Savior. William's countenance fell and guilt shown in his face, but his reply was a strong "no."

In the days that followed, William was quiet and his friend often felt that William was avoiding him. But one day the friend did receive a phone call from William, who wanted to knew where to look in the Bible for some verses about salvation. But he declined the friend's offer to meet with him. Obviously, William was troubled, but the friend didn't know where to reach him.

Because he was in training for the Olympic games, William had special privileges at the university's pool facilities. Some time late that evening after talking with his friend, William went to the pool to practice a few dives. It was a clear night in October and the moon was big and bright. The university pool was housed under a ceiling of glass panes so the moon shown bright across the wall in the pool area.

William climbed to the highest platform to take his first dive. At that moment, the Spirit of God began to convict him of his sins. All the scripture he had read, all the occasions his friend had witnessed to him flooded his mind.

He stood on the platform backwards to make his dive, spread his arms for balance, looked up to the wall and saw his own shadow caused by the light of the moon. It was the shape of a cross. He could bear the burden of his sin no longer. His heart broke and he sat down on the platform and asked God to forgive him and save him.

Suddenly, the lights in the pool area came on. The attendant had come in to check the pool. As William looked down from the platform he saw an empty pool which had been drained for repairs. He had almost dived to his death, but the cross had saved him from disaster.

Section VI

Touched by an E-mail

Tears and Laughter in School

The Extra Ribbon

A high school teacher wanted to honor each of her senior students by telling them the difference they each had made. After telling how each student made a difference to her and the class, she presented each of them with a blue ribbon imprinted with gold letters which read "It's Who I Am That Makes a Difference."

Later, the teacher decided to do a class project to see what kind of impact recognition would have on the community. She gave each of her students three more ribbons and instructed them to go out and and repeat the recognition ceremony with others.

One of the boys went to a junior executive in a nearby company and honored him for helping him with his career planning. He gave him a blue ribbon and pinned it to his shirt. Then he gave him two extra blue ribbons and said, "We're doing a class project on recognition, and we'd like you to go out, find somebody to honor, give them a blue ribbon to keep and an extra blue ribbon so they can acknowledge a third person to keep this recognition ceremony going.

Later that day, the junior executive went into see the boss, who had been noted as being kind of grouchy fellow. He sat his boss down and told him that he deeply admired him for his creative genius.

The boss seemed very surprised. The junior executive asked him if he would accept the gift of the blue ribbon and would he give permission to put it on him. His surprised boss said, "Well, sure." The junior executive took the blue ribbon and placed it right on his boss' jacket above his heart. As he gave him the last extra ribbon, he said, "Would you do me a favor? Would you take this extra ribbon and pass it on by honoring somebody else? The student who gave me the ribbons is doing a project in school and we want to keep this ceremony going.

That night the boss came home to his 14-year-old son and sat him down. He said, "The most incredible thing happened to me today.

"I was in my office and one of my junior executives came in and told me he admired me and gave me a blue ribbon for being a creative genius. Then he puts this blue ribbon on my jacket. He also gave me an extra ribbon and asked me to find someone else to honor.

"As I was driving home, I started thinking about whom I would honor with this ribbon and I thought about you. I want to honor you.

"My days are really hectic, and when I come home I don't pay a lot of attention to you. Sometimes I scream at you for not getting good grades and for your bedroom being a mess. But tonight, somehow, I just wanted to sit here and just let you know that you do make a difference to me. Besides your mother, you are the most important person in my life. You're a great kid and I love you."

The startled boy started to sob and he couldn't stop crying. His whole body shook. He looked at his father and said through his tears, "I was planning on committing suicide tomorrow, Dad, because I didn't think you loved me. "

Straight A's

A ten-year-old boy was failing math. His parents tried everything from tutors to hypnosis but to no avail. Finally, they decided to enroll their son in a private Christian school.

After the first day, the boy's parents were surprised when he walked in after school with a stern, focused and very determined expression on his face. He walked straight to his room.

For nearly two hours he toiled away in his room with math books spread about his desk and the surrounding floor. He came out long enough to eat and then went back to his room. He studied feverishly until it was time to go to bed. This pattern continued until it was time for the first quarter report card.

The boy walked in with his report card unopened, laid it on the dinner table and went straight to his room. Cautiously, his mother opened it and to her amazement, she saw a bright red "A" under the subject of MATH.

Overjoyed, she and her husband rushed to the boy's room, thrilled at his remarkable progress.

"Was it the wonderful teachers that did it?" the father said. The boy only shook his head and said, "No."

"Was it the one-on-one tutoring? The small classes?"

"No," the boy said.

"The textbooks? The curriculum? The new books?"

"Nope," said the son. "On that first day when I walked in the front door and saw that guy nailed to the "plus sign", I just knew they meant business."

Only in America

Only in America do people order double cheeseburgers, large fries and a diet soda.

Only in America do we leave cars worth thousands of dollars in the driveway and leave useless things and other junk in boxes in the garage.

Only in America do banks leave both doors open and then chain the pens to the counter.

Only in America can a pizza get to your house faster than an ambulance.

Only in America do we have several unread Bibles in our homes, while most of the people in other parts of the world are begging for just one copy.

And only in America – but not only America – can a school teacher get fired for having a Bible on her desk.

Changing Our Course

Several years ago at a Special Olympics track meet, nine contestants, all physically or mentally challenged, assembled at the starting line for the 100-yard dash. As the gun sounded, they all started out, not exactly in a dash, but with an excitement to run the race to the finish and win.

All, that is, except one boy who stumbled on the asphalt, tumbled over a couple of time and began to cry. The other eight heard the boy cry.

They slowed down and looked back. Then they all turned around and went back. Every one of them. One girl with Down's syndrome bent down and kissed him and said, "This will make it better." Then all nine linked arms and walked together to the finish line.

God's Arms Around You

Wishing to encourage her young son's progress on the piano, a mother took her boy to a Paderewski concert. After they were seated, the mother spotted a friend in the audience and walked down the aisle to greet her.

Seizing the opportunity to explore the wonders of the concert hall, the little boy rose and eventually explored his way through a door marked "NO ADMITTANCE." When the house lights dimmed and the concert was about to begin, the mother returned to her seat and discovered that the child was missing.

Suddenly, the curtains parted and spotlights focused on the impressive Steinway on stage. In horror, the mother saw her little boy sitting at the keyboard, innocently picking out "Twinkle, Twinkle Little Star."

At that moment, the great piano master made his entrance, quickly moved to the piano, and whispered in he boy's ear, "Don't quit. Keep playing." Then leaning over, Paderewski reached down with his left hand and began filling in a bass part. Soon his right arm reached around to the other side of the child and he added a running obbligato. Together, the old master and the young novice transformed a frightening situation into a wonderfully creative experience.

The audience was mesmerized.

That's the way it is with our Heavenly Father. What we can accomplish on our own is hardly noteworthy. We try our best, but the results aren't exactly graceful flowing music. But with the hand of the Master, our life's work truly can be beautiful. Next time you set out to accomplish great feats, listen carefully. You can hear the voice of the Master, whispering in your ear, "Don't quit. Keep playing."

Section VII

Touched by an E-mail

Tears and Laughter When Working

I Love You, Joe

Joe was driving home one evening on a two-lane country road. He'd been searching for a job with little success. Joe had been unemployed since the local clothing factory had closed, and things were really getting tight.

It was a lonely road, and he almost didn't see the elderly lady stranded on the side of the road. Even in the twilight, he could see she needed help. He pulled up by her Mercedes and stopped.

He knew he frightened her. He knew he didn't look safe. He tried to set her mind at ease. "I'm here to help you, ma'am. Why don't you wait in the car where it's warm. By the way, my name is Joe."

All she had was a flat tire, and Joe fixed it quickly even though he scraped his knuckles a few times trying to locate the jack under the car. The woman asked Joe how much she owed him. She had already imagined all the terrible things that could have happened had he not stopped to help her. But Joe never thought twice about the money. This was not a job to him. It was helping someone in need. He refused the money, thinking how many times people had given him a hand. Joe told the lady that if she really wanted to pay him back, the next time she saw someone who needed help, she could give that person the assistance they needed, and Joe added, ..."and think of me."

The woman drove off and a few miles down the road saw a small café where she could get a bite to eat. It was a dingy place, but she went inside.

Her waitress came over and brought her a clean towel to wipe her wet hair. The lady noticed the waitress was about eight months pregnant, but she never seemed to let the strain and aches change her attitude. She had a sweet smile, and the woman wondered how someone who had so little could be so giving to a stranger. Then she remembered Joe.

After the woman finished her meal, and the waitress went to get change for a $100 bill, the woman slipped out the door. She left a note on the napkin, which brought tears to the waitress' eyes when she read it. "Keep the change. You don't owe me a thing. I've been there, too. Someone once helped me out the way I'm helping you. If you really want to pay me back, don't let the chain of love end with you."

That night when the waitress got home from work she climbed into bed. She was thinking about the money and what the woman has written. How could she have known how much she and her husband needed it? With the baby due next month, it was going to be hard. She knew how worried her husband was, and as he lay sleeping next to her, she gave him a soft kiss and whispered, "Everything's going to be all right. I love you, Joe."

The Ten Dollar Loan

A man came home from work late again, tired and irritated, to find his five-year-old son waiting for him at the door. "Daddy, may I ask you a question?"

"Yeah, sure, what is it?" the man replied.

"Daddy, how much money do you make an hour"

"That's none of your business! What makes you ask such a thing," the father said angrily.

"I just want to know. Please tell me. How much do you make an hour?" pleaded the little boy.

"If you must know, I make $20 an hour."

"Oh," the boy replied, head bowed. Looking up, he said, "Daddy, may I borrow $10, please?"

The father was furious. "If the only reason you wanted to know how much money I make is just so you can borrow some to buy a silly toy, then you march yourself straight to your room and go to bed. Think about why you're being so selfish. I work long, hard hours everyday, and I don't have time for such childish games."

The little boy went quietly to his room and shut the door. The man sat down and started to get even more angry about the his son's questions.

How dare him ask such questions only to get some money, he thought.

After an hour or so, the father had calmed down, and he began to think he had been a little harsh on his son. Maybe there was something he really needed to buy with that $10, and he really didn't ask for money very often. The man went to the door of the boy's room and opened the door. "Are you asleep, son?" he asked.

"No, daddy, I'm awake," replied the boy.

"I've been thinking, maybe I was too hard on you earlier," the man said.

"It's been a long day and I took my aggravation out on you. Here's the $10 you asked for."

The little boy sat straight up, beaming. "Oh, thank you, daddy!" he yelled. Then reaching under his pillow, he pulled out some crumbled up bills. The man, seeing that the boy already had money, started to get angry again. The little boy slowly counted out his money, then looked up at his father.

"Why did you want more money if you already had some?" the father grumbled.

"Because I didn't have enough, but now I do," the little boy said.

"Daddy, I have $20 now. Can I buy an hour of your time?"

The Good Life

An American businessman was at the pier of a small coastal Mexican village when a small boat with just one fisherman docked.

Inside the boat were several large yellowfin tuna. The American complimented the Mexican on the quality of the fish and asked him how long it took to catch them. The Mexican told him it only took a little time. The American then asked why he didn't stay out longer and catch more fish. The Mexican said he had enough to support his family's immediate needs.

The American then asked, "But what do you do with the rest of your time?" And the Mexican said, "I sleep late, fish a little, play with my children, take siesta with my wife Maria, stroll into the village each evening where I sip wine and play guitar with my friends. I have a full and busy life, senor."

The American scoffed, "I am a Harvard MBA and could help you. You should spend more time fishing and with the proceeds buy a bigger boat. With the proceeds from the larger boat, you could buy several boats and eventually you would have a fleet of fishing boats. Instead of selling your catch to a middleman, you would sell directly to the processor, eventually opening your own cannery.

You could control the product, processing and distribution. You would need to leave this small coastal fishing village and move to Mexico City and then to Los Angeles and eventually to New York City, where you could run your expanding enterprise.

The Mexican fisherman asked, "But senor, how long will this all take?"

The American replied, "Probably 15 to 20 years."

"But what then, senor?"

The American laughed and said, "That's the best part. When the time is right you would sell stock in your company to the public and become very rich. You could make millions."

"Millions, senor? Then what?"

The American said, "Then you would retire. Move to a small coastal fishing village, where you would sleep late, fish a little, play with your kids, take siesta with your wife, stroll to the village in the evenings, where you could sip wine and play your guitar with your friends."

The Trouble Tree

I hired a carpenter to help me restore an old farmhouse. He had just finished a rough first day on the job: a flat tire made him lose an hour of work, the electric saw quit working, and now his pickup truck refused to start. While I drove him home, he sat in stony silence. On arriving, he invited me to meet his family.

As we walked toward the front door, he paused briefly at a small tree, touching the tips of the branches with both hands.

When opening the door he underwent an amazing transformation. His tanned face was wreathed in smiles and he hugged his two small children and gave his wife a kiss.

Afterwards he walked me to the car. We passed the tree and my curiosity got the better of me. I asked him about what I had seen him do earlier.

"Oh, that's my trouble tree," he replied. "I know I can't help having troubles on the job, but one thing is for sure, troubles don't belong in the house with my wife and the children. So I just hang them up on the tree every night when I come home. Then in the morning I pick them up again."

"Funny thing is," he smiled, "when I come out in the morning to pick them up, there aren't nearly as many as I remember hanging up the night before."

A Promise for A Promise

Many years ago, a young man prayed with his pastor and committed to God his tithe. His first week's pay was $10.00 and the tithe was $1.00.

As he grew older, the man became more prosperous and his tithe was $7.00 a week, then $10.00. He moved to another city and soon his tithe was $100 a week, then $200, then $500.

One day the man sent his old friend and pastor a letter. "Please come see me," he said. The pastor arrived at the man's house, and they had a good time talking over old times. Finally the man came to his point. "You remember that promise I made years ago to tithe? How can I get released?"

"Why would you want to get released?" asked the pastor.

"It's like this," the man answered. "When I made the promise I only had to give $1.00, but now it is $500. I can't afford to give away money like that."

The old pastor looked at his friend. "I'm afraid we cannot get released from the promise, but there is something we can do. We can kneel and ask God to shrink your income so you can afford to give $1.00 again."

Surrounded By Angels

A missionary was serving at a small field hospital in Africa. Every few weeks he traveled by bicycle through the jungle to a nearby city for supplies. His trip took two days, so he needed to camp overnight about halfway to his destination.

On one of his journeys to the city, he saw two men fighting, one of whom was seriously injured. He treated him for his injuries and at the same time talked to him about salvation. He then traveled back home without incident.

Two weeks later, he repeated the journey and upon arriving in the city was approached by the young man he had treated. He told the missionary that he knew he had been carrying money and medicine. "Some friends and I followed you into the jungle, knowing you would camp overnight. We planned to kill you and take your money and drugs. But just as we were about to move into your camp, we saw that you were surrounded by 26 armed guards."

At this, the missionary laughed and said that he was certainly all alone at his Camp, but the young man insisted that he and his friends had seen the guards and counted them.

Some time later during a sermon in the United States, the missionary was telling the story when one of the men in the congregation jumped to his feet and interrupted the missionary. He asked for the exact date of the incident. And then the man told this story:

"On the night of your incident in Africa, it was morning here and I was preparing to play golf. I was about to putt when I felt the urge to pray for you. In fact, the Lord's urging was so strong that I went and called the men in this church to meet me at the sanctuary to pray for you. Would all the men who met with me on that day stand up?" the man said.

The men who had met together to pray stood up. And when the missionary counted them, he saw that they numbered 26.

The Master Weaver

A missionary was traveling in the Far East when he came across a booth in a market place. It was a tapestry maker's booth. As he walked by he saw a strange sight. A man was standing in the booth shouting at his loom on the other side of the booth. As he shouted thread appeared in the tapestry almost by magic. The missionary asked his guide for an explanation.

"The man you see," said the guide, "is a master weaver. He is speaking to his apprentice behind the loom telling him what color thread to use and where to put it. Only the weaver knows the entire design, so it is vital that the apprentice does exactly as the master commands."

"Does the apprentice ever make a mistake?" asked the missionary.

"Of course, but the weaver is a very kind man. He will rarely have the boy take out the thread. Instead, being a great artist, he simply works the mistake into the design."

How much that is like God. We cannot see the pattern of the tapestry God is weaving. We are on the other side of the loom looking at knotted threads placed seemingly without purpose. Occasionally, we can catch a glimpse of the design, but then as soon as we think we understand it, the master calls for a thread which changes everything.

So we have to trust the master weaver that he knows what he is doing.

And like the apprentice, we also make mistakes. We put in a red thread instead of a violet one. We knot it in the wrong place or place it in a crooked way. And God in His mercy doesn't criticize us but takes our mistakes and makes them part of the design.

How God's Leaders Lead

More by listening than by what we say;
More by being than by doing;
More by allowing things to happen than
   making them happen;
More by surrendering than by being in control;
More by accepting than by comparing;
More from the heart than from the head;
More by internal change than by external
   change;
And more by being rooted in who we are rather
   than according to the reactions of others.

Cracked Pots

A water-bearer in India had two large pots, each hung on one end of a pole which he carried across his shoulders. One of the pots had a crack in it, but the other pot was perfect. The perfect pot always delivered a full portion of water at the end of the long walk from the stream to the master's house. The cracked pot arrived only half full.

This went on daily for two years with the bearer delivering only one and one-half pot of water to his master's house.

Of course the perfect pot was proud of its accomplishments. But the poor cracked pot was ashamed of its own imperfection and miserable that it was able to accomplish only half of what it had been made to do.

After two years of what it perceived to be a bitter failure, it spoke to the water-bearer. "I am ashamed of myself, and I want to apologize to you." "Why?" asked the bearer. "What are you ashamed of?"

"For the past two years," the pot said, "I have been able to deliver only half my load because this crack allows the water to leak out as we travel. You don't get full value for your efforts."

The water-bearer felt sorry for the old cracked pot, and in his compassion he said, "As we return to the master's house, I want you to notice the beautiful flowers along the path." Indeed, as they went up the hill, the cracked pot took notice of the sun warming the beautiful wild flowers on the side of the path. This cheered it some, but at the end of the trail, it still felt bad because it had leaked out half its load.

The bearer said to the pot, "Did you notice that there were flowers only on your side of the path, but not on the perfect pot's side? That's because I have always known of your flow, and I took advantage of it.

I planted flower seeds on your side of the path, and every day while we walk back from the stream, you've watered them. For two years I've been able to pick these beautiful flowers to decorate my master's table.

Without you being just the way you are, he would not have this beauty to grace his house."

Each of us has our unique flaws. We're all cracked pots. But if we will allow it, the Lord will use our flaws to grace His Father's table.

Hardly Reassuring

There is a story about a monastery in Europe perched high on a cliff several hundred feet in the air. The only way to reach the monastery was to be suspended in a basket which was lifted to the top of the cliff by several monks who tugged and tugged.

Obviously the ride up the steep cliff was terrifying. One tourist got exceedingly nervous about half-way up as he noticed that the rope by which he was suspended was old and frayed.

With a trembling voice, he asked the monk who was riding with him in the basket how often they changed the rope.

The monk thought for a moment and answered brusquely, "Whenever it breaks."

Every Woman Should Know

- How to fall in love without losing yourself.
- How you feel about having kids.
- How to quit a job, break up with a man, and confront a friend without ruining the friendship.
- When to try harder and when to walk away.
- How to have a good time at a party you'd never choose to attend.

- How to ask for what you want in a way that makes it most likely you'll get it.
- That you can't change the length of your calves, the width of your hips, or the nature of your parents.
- That your childhood may not have been perfect, but it's over.
- How to live alone, even if you don't like it.
- Who you can trust, who you can't, and why you shouldn't take it personally.

Section VIII

Touched by an E-mail

Tears and Laughter at the Pearly Gates

The View Outside

Two seriously ill men occupied the same hospital room. One man was allowed to sit up in his bed a few hours a day. His bed was next to the room's only window. The other man had to spend all his time flat on his back. The men talked together for hours on end. And every afternoon when the man by the window sat up, he would pass the time by describing to his roommate all the things he could see outside the window.

The man in the other bed would live for those hours when his world would be broadened and enlivened by all the activity and color of the outside world. The window overlooked a park with a lovely lake. The man described how ducks and swans played on the water, how children sailed their little boats, and how lovers walked arm-in-arm amid flowers of every color. As the man by the window described all this, the man on the other side of the room would close his eyes and imagine the beautiful scene.

One warm afternoon, as the view outside was being described, an unsettling thought entered the mind of the man who was listening. Why should the other man have all the pleasure of seeing everything, while I never get to see anything? It didn't seem fair. As the thought fermented, the man felt ashamed at first. But as the days passed and he missed seeing more sights, his envy eroded into resentment and soon he turned sour. He began to brood and found himself unable to sleep. He should be by that window was the thought that now controlled his life.

It wasn't long after that that the man by the window died during his sleep.

As soon as it seemed appropriate, the other man asked if he could be moved next to the window. The nurse was happy to make the switch and after making sure he was comfortable she left him alone. Slowly, painfully, he propped himself up on one elbow to take his first look. Finally, he would have the joy of seeing it all himself. He strained to slowly turn to look out the window beside the bed....It faced a blank wall.

God Is Good

An elderly man has loved God all his life, and he often walked around saying "God is good." He said it whenever and wherever he was. When he got married, he said "God is good." When he lost his job, he said "God is good."

When his father died, he said "God is good." It was apparent to everyone around him. No matter what he did, no matter what happened to him, they would hear him say "God is good."

A few months ago, the man was diagnosed with terminal cancer. Sadly, his doctor told him he had but a few weeks to live. Still, even on his deathbed, he could be heard by everyone in the hospital repeating "God is good." The man's pastor was his best friend and every time the pastor visited the hospital, he would hear the same welcoming and parting words, "God is good."

Finally, the pastor had to ask his friend. He said, "You are my best friend and I love you. I love the Lord as much as you do, too. I have listened to you say 'God is good' your whole life. Through the good times, I can understand you saying 'God is good.' Maybe even during the hard times to help you cope. But now, laying here on the deathbed, how can you be so optimistic? How can you say God is good every day when you know he is letting you die?" The man just looked at his pastor and smiled.

"My friend," he whispered, " don't you see all those times I was saying God is good, it was my way of praising Him in every way I could. And look what my reward is for remaining faithful. I am dying. You say God is letting me die as if that is a bad thing. I think you have forgotten that is our goal. To live our life for Him, and join Him one day in heaven. See,

God is good! He has finally called me home and in a few hours I will be with Him. I can't imagine anything greater than that."

The man died that night in his sleep. At the funeral, his friend and pastor said only two things. "I will miss my friend, but I know I will see him again one day soon. And God is good."

Something Better For Edna

An elderly woman named Edna was in the hospital, approaching her last days. She had no family, and so she called her pastor and asked him to discuss with her what she wanted in her funeral service. She told him the songs she wanted, the scriptures she wanted, and the clothes she wanted. She also said she wanted to be buried with her favorite Bible. Then she said, "There is something else I want done that is very important to me, but I don't want you to think I'm just a silly old woman."

The pastor smiled, "I won't think that, Edna."

Edna hesitated a moment and then said, "I want to be buried with a dinner fork in my hand."

The pastor tried not to look like he thought Edna as a silly old woman, but he didn't know what to say. "That shocks you doesn't it?" Edna asked.

"Well, to be honest, Edna," said the pastor, "I am puzzled by your request."

Edna explained. "In all my years of attending our church socials and functions where food was served, my favorite part was when whoever was clearing away the dishes of the main course would lean over me and say, 'Edna, keep your fork.' It was my favorite part because I knew that something better was coming. When they told me to keep my fork I knew that something really good and tasty was about to be served. It wasn't going to be pudding or something soft. It was going to be pie or cake – something with substance. So I want people to see me in the casket with a fork in my hand so they'll ask, 'Why does Edna have a fork in her hand. When they do, I want you to tell them, 'Something better is coming for Edna.' Then tell them they should keep their folks, too.

The pastor's eyes welled with tears of joy as he hugged Edna. He knew this would probably be one of the last times he would see Edna. But he also knew that Edna had a better grasp of heaven than he did. She knew something better was coming.

At the funeral, some of those who stopped at Edna's casket commented on her pretty dress or said something about her favorite Bible. But everyone asked, "Why does she have a fork in her hand?" And every time they asked, the pastor enjoyed telling them that "something better is coming for Edna."

Things aren't Always What They Seem

Two traveling angels stopped to spend the night in the home of a wealthy family. The family was rude and refused to let the angels stay in the mansion's guest room. Instead, the angels were given a small space in the cold basement. As they made their bed on the hard floor, the older angel saw a hole in the wall and repaired it.

When the younger angel asked why, the older angel replied, "Things aren't always what they seem."

The next night the pair came to rest at the house of a very poor, but very hospitable farmer and his wife. After sharing what little food they had, the couple let the angels sleep in their bed where they could have a good night's rest.

When the sun came up the next morning, the angels found the farmer and his wife in tears. Their only cow, whose milk had been their sole income, lay dead in the field. The younger angel was infuriated and asked the older angel how he could have let this happen. "The first man had everything, yet you helped him," the young angel said. "The second family had little but was willing to share everything, and you let the cow die.

"Things aren't always what they seem," the older angel replied.

"When we stayed in the basement of the mansion, I noticed there was gold stored in the hole in the wall. Since the owner was so obsessed with greed and unwilling to share his good fortune, I sealed the wall so he wouldn't find it.

"Then last night as we slept in the farmer's bed, the angel of death came for his wife. I gave him the cow instead. Things aren't always what they seem."

The Chair By the Bed

A man's daughter had asked the local pastor to come and pray with her father. When he arrived, he found the man lying in bed with his head propped up on two pillows and an empty chair beside his bed. The pastor assumed that the old fellow had been informed of his visit. "I guess you were expecting me," he said.

"No. who are you?"

"Oh, the chair," said the bedridden man. "Would you mind closing the door?"

Puzzled, the pastor shut the door.

"I've never told anyone this, not even my daughter," said the man. "But all of my life I have never known how to pray. At church services I used to hear the pastor talk about prayer, but it always went right over my head.

I abandoned any attempt at prayer," the old man continued, "until one day my best friend said to me, 'Joe, prayer is just a simple matter of having a conversation with Jesus. Here's what I suggest. Sit down on a chair, place an empty chair in front of you, and in faith see Jesus on the chair.

'He promised, 'I'll be with you always.' Just speak to Him and listen in the same way you're doing with me right now.' So, I tried it and liked it so much that I do it a couple of days every day. I'm careful, though.

If my daughter saw me talking to an empty chair, she either have a nervous breakdown or send me off to the funny farm."

The pastor was deeply moved by the story and encouraged the man to continue on the journey. Then he prayed with him, anointed him, and left.

Two nights later, the daughter called to tell the Pastor that her daddy had died that afternoon. "Did he seem to die in peace?" he asked.

"Yes, the daughter said. "When I left the house, he called me over to his bedside, told me one of his corny jokes, and kissed me on the cheek.

When I got back an hour later, I found him dead. But there was something strange. Apparently, just before daddy died, he leaned over and rested his head on a chair beside the bed."

You Look Like A New Woman

A middle-aged woman has a heart attack and is taken to the hospital. While on the operating table she has a near-death experience.

During the experience, she sees God and asks if this is the end. God says "no" and explains that she has another 30 to 40 years to live.

Upon her recovery, the woman decides to stay in the hospital and have a face lift, liposuction, tummy tuck and other "improvements."

She even has someone change her hair color. She figures she might as well make the best of another 30 to 40 years.

She walks out of the hospital after the last operation and is killed by an ambulance speeding up to the emergency room door.

She arrives in front of God and asks, "I thought you said I had another 30 to 40 years." But God replies, "I guess I didn't recognize you."

The Life Long Dash

I read of a man who stood to speak
At the funeral of a friend.
He referred to the dates on her tombstone
From the beginning to the end.

He noted that first came the date of her birth
And spoke of the following date with tears,
But he said what mattered most of all
Was the dash between those years.

For that represents all the time
That she spent alive on earth.
And now only those who loved her
Know what that little line is worth.

For it matters not, how much we own;
The cars, the house, the cash.
What matters is how we live and love
And how we spend our dash.

So think about this long and hard.
Are there things you'd like to change?
For you never know how much time is left.
You could be at dash mid-range.

If we treat each other with respect,
And more often wear a smile.
Remembering that this special dash
Might last just a little while.

So when your eulogy's being read
With your life's actions to rehash,
Would you be proud of the things they say
About how you spent your dash?

Miss Me, But Let Me Go

When I come to the end of the road
    And the sun has set for me
I want no rites in a gloom-filled room.
    Why cry for a soul set free?

Miss me a little, but not too long
    And not with your head bowed low.
Remember the love that we once shared,
    Miss me, but let me go.

For this is a journey that we all must take
    And each must go alone.
It's all a part of the Master's plan,
    A step on the road to home.

When you are lonely and sick of heart
  Go to the friends we know
And bury your sorrows in doing good deeds,
  Miss me, but let me go.

God's Scorecard

A man dies and goes to heaven, where St. Peter meets him at the Pearly Gates. St. Peter says, "Here's how it works. You need 100 points to get into heaven. You tell me all the good things you've done, and I'll give you a certain number of points for each item, depending upon how good it was. When you reach 100 points, you can come in."

"Okay," the man says, "I was married to the same woman for 50 years and never cheated on her, even in my heart."

"That's wonderful," St. Peter said, "that's worth three points."

"Three points?" the man says. "Well, I attended church all my life and supported its ministry with my tithe and service."

"Terrific!" says St. Peter, "that's certainly worth a point."

"One point? Golly. How about this? I started a soup kitchen in my city and worked in a shelter for homeless veterans."

"Fantastic, that's good for two more points," St. Peter says.

"Two points!" the man cries, "at this rate the only way I get into heaven is by the grace of God."

St. Peter smiles and says, "Come on in."

He's Upstairs

A doctor who had devoted his life to helping the underprivileged lived over a liquor store in the poor section of a large city. In front of the liquor store was a simple sign reading "Dr. Williams is upstairs."

When he died, the doctor had no relatives and he left no money for his burial. He had never asked for payment from anyone he had ever treated. Friends and patients scraped together enough money to bury the good doctor, but they had no money for a tombstone. It appeared his grave was going to be unmarked until someone came up with a wonderful suggestion.

They took the sign from in front of the liquor store and nailed it to a post over his grave. It made a lovely epitaph: Dr. Williams is upstairs.

The Tire Iron Guy

A guy is at the Pearly Gates, waiting to be admitted, while St. Peter looks through the "Big Book of Life" to see if the fellow is worthy of entering.

St. Peter goes through the book several times, furrows his brow, and says to the man, "You know, I can't see that you did anything really good in your life, but you never did anything really bad either. Tell you what, if you can tell me of one really good deed that you did in your life, you're in."

The guy thinks for a moment and says, "Yeah, there was this one time when I was driving down the highway and I saw a giant biker gang hassling this poor girl. I slowed my car down to see what was going on and sure enough, there they were, about 50 of them, harassing this young woman. So I got out of my car, grabbed a tire iron out of my trunk, and walked straight up to the leader of the gang. He was huge guy with a studded leather jacket and a chain running from his nose to his ear. As I walked up to the leader, the entire gang formed a circle around me.

"Anyway, I ripped the leader's chain off his face and smashed him over the head with the tire iron. Then I turned around and yelled at the rest of them, 'Leave this poor, innocent girl alone. You're a bunch of sick, deranged animals. Go home before I teach you all a lesson in pain."

St. Peter, impressed, asks. "Really? When did this happen?"

"Oh, about two minutes ago."

Heavenly Surprise

I dreamed that death came the other night
And heaven's gate swung wide;
With kindly grace and angel came
To usher me inside.

Yet there to my astonishment
Stood folks I'd known on earth,
Some I had judged as quite unfit
Or of but little worth.

Indignant words rose to my lips
But never were set free;
For every face showed stunned surprise
No one expected me!

I Need To Phone Heaven

Mommy went to Heaven, but I need her here today.

My tummy hurts and I fell down. I need her right away.

Operator can you tell me how to find her in this book?

Is Heaven in the yellow part? I don't know where to look.

I think my daddy needs her, too. At night I hear him cry.

I hear him call her name sometimes, but I really don't know why.

Maybe if I call her she will hurry home to me.

Is Heaven very far away? Is it across the sea?

She's been gone a long, long time. She needs to come home now.

I really need to reach her, but I simply don't know how.

Help me find the number, please. Is it listed under "Heaven?"

I can't read these big, big words. I am only seven.

I'm sorry, operator. I didn't mean to make you cry.

Is your tummy hurting, too, or is something in your eye?

If I call my church maybe they will know.

Mommy said when we need help that's where we should go.

I found the number to my church tacked up on the wall.

Thank you, operator. I'll give them a call.

God Will Love Those Shoes

It was just a few days before Christmas. The discount store was jammed with last-minute shoppers. "Why did I come here, today?" the woman asked herself.

Hurriedly, she filled her basket with the final gifts on her list and headed toward the long check-out lines. In front of her were two small children – a boy about five and a younger girl. They wore dirty, ragged clothing and old shoes several sizes too large. The boy clutched several crumpled dollar bills in his hand, and the little girl carried a beautiful pair of shiny, gold house slippers.

When we finally approached the checkout register, the girl placed the shoes on the counter. She treated them as if they were a treasure.

The clerk rang up the bill. "That will be $6.09," she said. The boy laid his crumbled money on the counter while he searched his pockets. He finally came up with $3.12. "I guess we'll have to put them back," he bravely said.

"We will come back some other time, maybe tomorrow." With that statement, a soft sob came from the little girl. "But God would have loved these shoes," she cried. "Well," the boy said, "we'll go home and work some more. Don't cry. We'll come back."

Quickly the woman handed $3.00 to the cashier. The children had waited in line for a long time. After all, she thought, it's Christmas. Suddenly a pair of arms came around her and a small voice said, "Thank you, lady."

"What do you mean when you said God would like the shoes," she asked.

The boy answered, "Our mommy is sick and going to heaven. Daddy said she might go before

Christmas to be with God." The girl spoke, "My Sunday school teacher said the streets in heaven are shiny gold, just like these shoes. Won't mommy be beautiful walking on those streets in these slippers?"

The woman's eyes flooded as she looked into the girl's tear-streaked face. "Yes," she answered, "I'm sure she will."

Don't You Care

The day is over. You are driving home listening to your radio. There's a brief news item about some villagers in India dying suddenly of a new flu-like disease.

The U.S. is sending some doctors to investigate.

You don't think much about it until the next day when you hear another broadcast. It wasn't three dead villagers, it was 30,000. The disease strain has never been seen before.

By the next day, you hear that the disease has spread through the Middle East.

It's being called the "mystery flu," and the President is asking everyone to pray for the many sick and dying people in the world. But everyone is wondering, how can we keep it from spreading?

The President of France has closed the borders, but a case has been found in Paris. Britain closes its borders also, but it's too late. The disease is deadly, and most people die within four to five days.

Finally, the United States closes its borders, but the nation is plunged into unbelievable fear and panic. You are at a church prayer meeting the next evening when someone runs in and announces that two women in Long Island have contracted the disease. Within hours, it seems, this thing sweeps across the country.

Researchers are working like crazy to find a vaccine. Then the sudden news comes that the code has been broken. A vaccine has been developed. But the process requires the blood of someone who hasn't been infected or exposed to the disease. In every state, people are asked to take blood tests, so the right blood can be found.

You take your family to the hospital to be tested. They test your blood and that of your wife and son and you're told to wait. Soon, a doctor comes running up to you. He grabs your boy and tells you his blood is perfect "You son can save the world," he yells.

You are quite pleased until the doctor asks you to sign a consent form. You begin to sign but notice that the line where it describes how many pints are to be taken has been left blank. "How many pints?" you ask.

And that is when the doctor's smile fades and he says, "We had no idea it would be a little child. We weren't prepared. We need all his blood, sir."

As the father objects, the doctor pleads with him. "We are talking about the whole world here," he says. "Please sign."

In numb silence, you do sign. Then they say, "Would you like a moment with him before we begin?

You find him sitting on a table. "Mommy, Daddy," he says, "What's going on?"

You take his hands in yours and tell him, "Son, we love you very much. We would never let anything happen to you that didn't just have to be.

The doctor reappears and says, "I'm sorry, but we have to get started. People all over the world are dying."

The following week when they have the memorial ceremony to honor your son, some of your friends don't come. They're too busy. Others show up but fall asleep halfway through the service. Others show up obviously because they believe it's politically correct to be seen there.

And you just want to stand up and scream: "My son died for you! Don't you care?"

Is that what God is saying today? "My son died for you! Don't you know how much I care?"